# It's another Quality Book from CGP

This book has been carefully written for 7-8 year olds.

It contains lots of questions covering all the Maths in the Year 3 Programme of Study — all perfectly matched to the National Curriculum for 2014 and beyond.

There are also practice tests at the start and end of the book to make sure you really know your stuff.

# What CGP is all about

Our sole aim here at CGP is to produce the highest quality books — carefully written, immaculately presented and dangerously close to being funny.

Then we work our socks off to get them out to you — at the cheapest possible prices.

# Contents

About This Book ..................................................................1

Year Two Objectives Test ......................................................2

## Section One — Number and Place Value

Place Value ......................................................................6
Reading and Writing Numbers ............................................7
Counting in Multiples ........................................................8
10 or 100 More or Less ....................................................9
Ordering and Comparing Numbers....................................10
Partitioning ....................................................................12
Numbers on Scales ........................................................14
Solving Number Problems................................................16

## Section Two — Calculations

Mental Addition ..............................................................18
Mental Subtraction..........................................................19
Written Addition..............................................................20
Written Subtraction ........................................................21
The 3, 4 and 8 Times Tables..........................................22
Using Times Tables Facts ...............................................23
Estimating and Checking ................................................25
Solving Calculation Problems...........................................26

## Section Three — Fractions

Counting in Tenths .........................................................28
Equivalent Fractions .......................................................29
Ordering Fractions..........................................................30
Adding and Subtracting Fractions ....................................32
Fractions of Amounts .....................................................34
Solving Fraction Problems ..............................................36

## Section Four — Measurement

Length, Mass and Volume......................................................38
Perimeter....................................................................40
Money.........................................................................42
Clocks........................................................................43
Time Problems................................................................44

## Section Five — Geometry

2D Shapes....................................................................46
3D Shapes....................................................................48
Angles and Lines.............................................................50

## Section Six — Statistics

Tables.......................................................................52
Bar Charts...................................................................53
Pictograms...................................................................54
Interpreting Tables and Charts...............................................55


Year Three Objectives Test..................................................56

Answers......................................................................60

Published by CGP

*Editors:*
Katie Braid, Katherine Craig, Rob Harrison, Sarah Pattison, Camilla Simson.

*Contributor:*
Simon Greaves

ISBN: 978 1 84762 211 2

*With thanks to Ben Fletcher and Nicola Paddock for the proofreading.*
*Also thanks to Jan Greenway for the copyright research.*

*Thumb illustration used throughout the book © iStockphoto.com.*

*Contains public sector information licensed under the Open Government Licence v2.0.*
*http://www.nationalarchives.gov.uk/doc/open-government-licence/*

Printed by Elanders Ltd, Newcastle upon Tyne.
Clipart from Corel®

Based on the classic CGP style created by Richard Parsons.

Text, design, layout and original illustrations © Coordination Group Publications Ltd. (CGP) 2014
All rights reserved.

**Photocopying this book is not permitted. Extra copies are available from CGP with next day delivery.**
**0800 1712 712 • www.cgpbooks.co.uk**

# About This Book

## This Book is Full of Year 3 Maths Questions

You'll learn a lot of <u>new maths</u> in Year 3.
This book has questions on <u>all the maths</u> for
Year 3. It <u>matches</u> our <u>Year 3 Study Book</u>.
This can help you if you get stuck.

*This book covers the <u>Attainment Targets</u> for <u>Year 3</u> of the <u>2014 National Curriculum</u>. The topics covered are roughly equivalent to the <u>old Levels 2-3</u>.*

The questions in Sections 1-6 are all <u>colour-coded</u> to show how <u>difficult</u> they are.

① Easy  ② Harder  ③ Challenge

The <u>answers</u> to all of the questions are at the <u>back of this book</u>.

This book also has <u>two Objectives Tests</u>.

The one at the <u>front of the book</u> is to test that you <u>remember</u> the maths you learnt in <u>Year 2</u>. The test at the <u>back of the book</u> is to see how well you know the maths in <u>this book</u>.

## There are Learning Objectives on All Pages

Learning objectives say <u>what you should be able to do</u>.
Use the <u>tick circles</u> to show how <u>confident</u> you feel.

*I can win silver at the Olympics.*

*You can use the tick boxes for <u>ongoing assessment</u> to record which <u>attainment targets</u> have been met. <u>Printable checklists</u> of all the objectives can be found at www.cgpbooks.co.uk/primarymaths.*

If you're really struggling, tick here.

Tick here if you think you need a bit more practice.

Tick this circle if you can do all the maths on the page.

"I can subtract 1s, 10s and 100s from a 3-digit number."

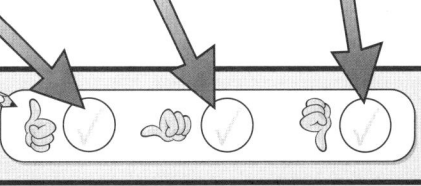

ABOUT THIS BOOK

# Year Two Objectives Test

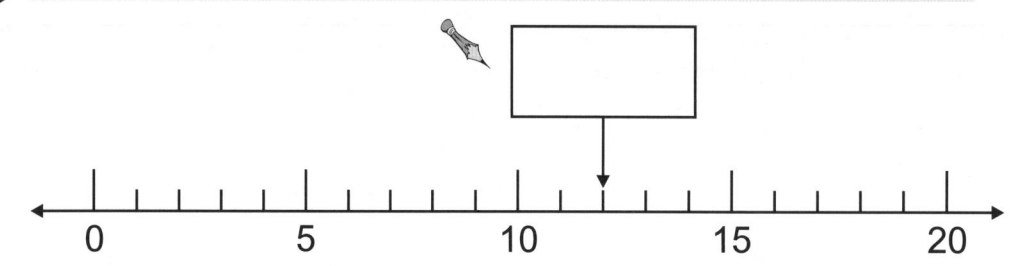

**1** Look at this number line. What number is the arrow pointing to?

1 mark

**2** What is the value of the 4 in 48?

1 mark

**3** Wilbur is writing a cheque for £89. Write this amount in words.

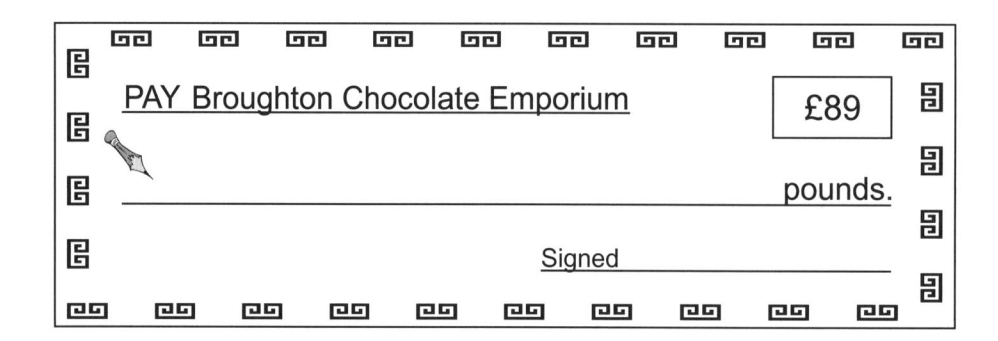

PAY Broughton Chocolate Emporium   £89

_____ pounds.

Signed _____

1 mark

**4** Draw a line of symmetry on this shape.

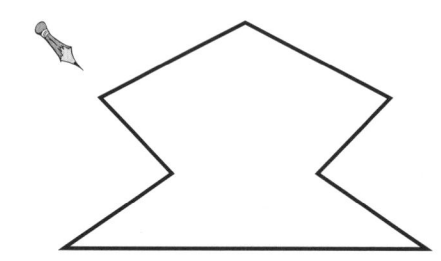

1 mark

**5** Ash is counting up in steps of 3. Fill in the next three numbers.

3   6   9   12   ☐   ☐   ☐

1 mark

**6** Calculate these sums.

3 + 7

☐

1 mark

20 + 60

☐

1 mark

**7** Look at this 3D shape.

How many faces does it have? ☐

1 mark

How many vertices does it have? ☐

1 mark

**8** Ashley counted the number of bats she saw in her garden each night. The pictogram shows how many bats she saw on three nights.

Monday   ○ ◐
Tuesday   ○ ○ ○ ◐
Wednesday ○ ○ ○

Key:
○ = 2 bats

How many bats did Ashley see on Tuesday? ☐ bats

1 mark

*Year Two Objectives Test*

**9** Robin wants to know how long his pet goldfish is.
Circle the units he should use to measure it.

kg    ml    m
  cm    g

**10** Look at this shape.

Circle the picture below that shows the shape after a right angle turn.

**11** Jeanette's birthday party starts at quarter past six.
Show this time on the clock by drawing where the hands should be.

**12** Hamish says that 56 + 23 = 79.

Write down an inverse calculation that you could use to check his answer.

**13** Tom calculates 4 × 2. He then adds 5 to this number.

What is Tom's final answer?

**14** Sasha has 15 roses and 3 vases.

She puts the same number of roses in each vase.
How many roses are in each vase?

_____ roses

**15** Write < or > to fill in the box.

41 ☐ 36

**16** Josh has a bag of 12 sweets.

What is $\frac{1}{2}$ of 12? Circle the correct answer.

4    2    3    10    6    24    9

Annie has 24 sweets. She gives $\frac{1}{3}$ of them to Josh.
How many sweets does she give to Josh?

_____ sweets

**17** Calculate 54 – 23.

YEAR TWO OBJECTIVES TEST

# Section One — Number and Place Value

# Place Value

**1)** Write down how many hundreds are in each number.

356 ▢     723 ▢

*2 marks*

**2)** Write down the digit in the tens place of each of these numbers.

76 ▢     903 ▢

*2 marks*

**3)** Write down the digit in the ones place of each of these numbers.

74 ▢     851 ▢

*2 marks*

**4)** Here are some number cards.

| 1 | 7 | 5 |

Rearrange the cards to get a number with:

5 hundreds ▢     5 tens ▢

*2 marks*

**5)** What is the value of the 3 in the number 234?

▢

*1 mark*

"I can recognise the place value of each digit in a three-digit number (hundreds, tens and ones)."

Section One — Number and Place Value

# Reading and Writing Numbers

**1** Write these numbers as numerals.

six hundred and eighty

nine hundred and sixty two

four hundred and one

**2** Write these numbers in words.

709

222

1000

**3** Jimmy has four cats. He is given five more. How many cats does he have now?

Write your answer in words.

cats

"I can read and write numbers up to 1000 in numerals and in words."

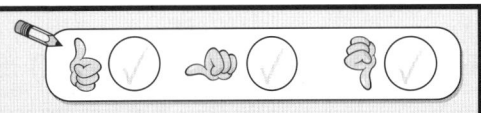

SECTION ONE — NUMBER AND PLACE VALUE

# Counting in Multiples

**1** List the first 5 multiples of 4.

One has been done for you.

4 , ☐ , ☐ , ☐ , ☐

1 mark

**2** List the first 5 multiples of 100.

100 , ☐ , ☐ , ☐ , ☐

1 mark

**3** Circle the multiples of 50.

100    500    36    120    250

1 mark

**4** Look at the digit cards:

| 1 | 2 | 4 | 0 | 5 | 0 |

Use 2 cards to make:

a two-digit multiple of 8. ☐    a two-digit multiple of 4. ☐

Use 3 cards to make:

a three-digit multiple of 100. ☐    a three-digit multiple of 50. ☐

2 marks

**5** Put a number less than 30 in each section of the table.

|  | multiple of 8 | not a multiple of 8 |
|---|---|---|
| multiple of 4 |  |  |

2 marks

"I can count in multiples of 4, 8, 50 and 100."

SECTION ONE — NUMBER AND PLACE VALUE

# 10 or 100 More or Less

**1)** Write in the number that is 10 more than:

649    one hundred and eighty

2 marks

**2)** Jackie has 116 coins. Kate has 10 less.

How many coins does Kate have?

1 mark

**3)** Write in the missing numbers.

100 less than 233    100 more than four hundred and thirty

2 marks

**4)** Write in the missing numbers.

10 less than 604    10 more than 896

2 marks

**5)** Match the numbers which have a difference of 10.
One has been done for you.

22          172
96          12
182         106
75          91
101         85

2 marks

"I can find 10 or 100 more than a number, and 10 or 100 less than a number."

SECTION ONE — NUMBER AND PLACE VALUE

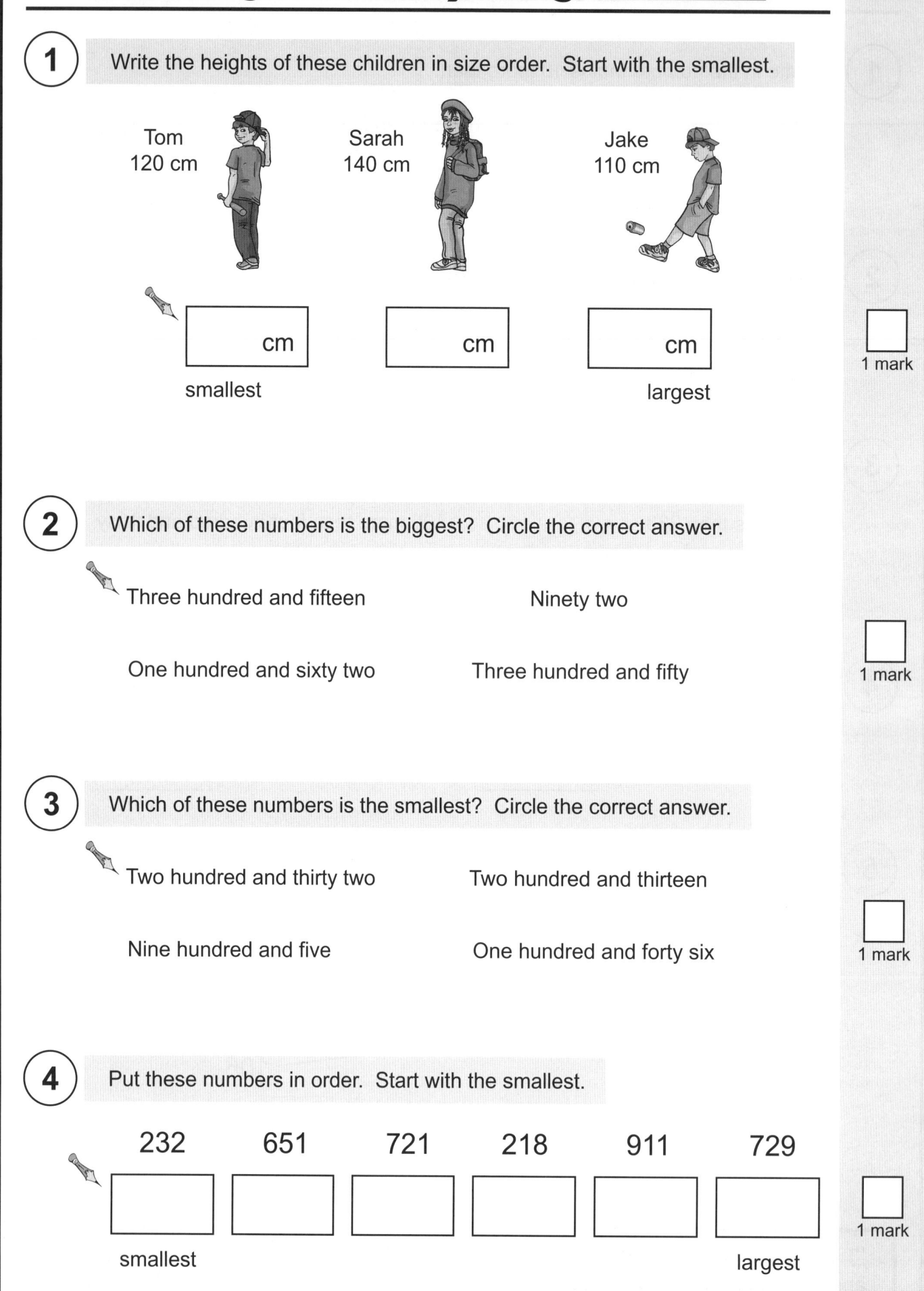

# Ordering and Comparing Numbers

**1** Write the heights of these children in size order. Start with the smallest.

Tom 120 cm    Sarah 140 cm    Jake 110 cm

[ 110 cm ] smallest    [ 120 cm ]    [ 140 cm ] largest

1 mark

**2** Which of these numbers is the biggest? Circle the correct answer.

Three hundred and fifteen        Ninety two

One hundred and sixty two        Three hundred and fifty

1 mark

**3** Which of these numbers is the smallest? Circle the correct answer.

Two hundred and thirty two        Two hundred and thirteen

Nine hundred and five             One hundred and forty six

1 mark

**4** Put these numbers in order. Start with the smallest.

232    651    721    218    911    729

[   ] [   ] [   ] [   ] [   ] [   ]
smallest                    largest

1 mark

SECTION ONE — NUMBER AND PLACE VALUE

# Ordering and Comparing Numbers

**5** Look at these prices.

Cheesecake 159p

Chocolate Mousse 98p

Sundae 153p

Write the amounts in order. Start with the largest amount.

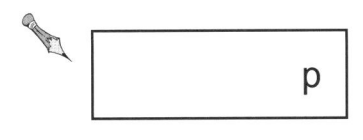

[ ] p    [ ] p    [ ] p

largest                                smallest

1 mark

**6** Look at these temperatures. Write < or > in each box.

21 °C [ ] 23 °C     13 °C [ ] 3 °C

7 °C [ ] 5 °C     0 °C [ ] 1 °C

2 marks

**7** Using <, > or =, fill in the boxes.

7 + 11 [ ] 6 + 4     6 + 8 [ ] 7 + 7

5 + 8 [ ] 2 + 9     9 − 8 [ ] 9 − 6

2 marks

"I can compare and order numbers up to 1000."

SECTION ONE — NUMBER AND PLACE VALUE

# Partitioning

**1)** Fill in the totals.

300 + 60 + 7 = ☐   100 + 10 + 9 = ☐

700 + 30 + 5 = ☐   200 + 50 + 8 = ☐

*2 marks*

**2)** Partition these numbers into hundreds, tens and ones.

438 = ☐ + ☐ + ☐   *1 mark*

652 = ☐ + ☐ + ☐   *1 mark*

109 = ☐ + ☐ + ☐   *1 mark*

**3)** Fill in the boxes to make these sums correct.

250 + ☐ + ☐ = 400   *1 mark*

420 + ☐ + ☐ = 600   *1 mark*

680 + ☐ + ☐ = 1000   *1 mark*

SECTION ONE — NUMBER AND PLACE VALUE

# Partitioning

**4** Use partitioning to do the following sums:

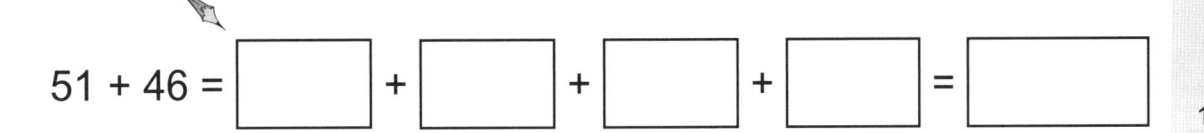

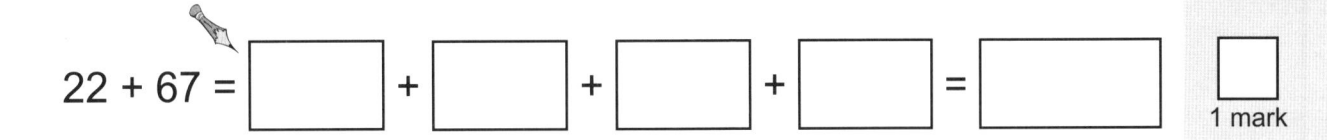

51 + 46 = ☐ + ☐ + ☐ + ☐ = ☐   1 mark

22 + 67 = ☐ + ☐ + ☐ + ☐ = ☐   1 mark

**5** Sophie's bus has 17 passengers. 21 more people get on.

How many passengers are there on the bus now?

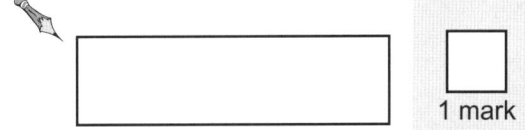

☐   1 mark

**6** Mr Green buys 2 boxes of chocolates containing 32 chocolates each.

How many chocolates does Mr Green have in total?

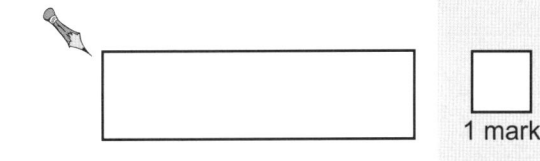

☐   1 mark

**7** Dennis goes for a walk. It takes him 20 minutes to get to the shop, 14 minutes to reach the river, then 6 minutes to get home.

How long does Dennis' walk take him in total?

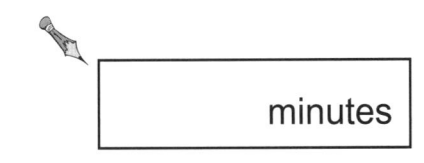

☐ minutes   1 mark

"I can use partitioning to show numbers in different ways."

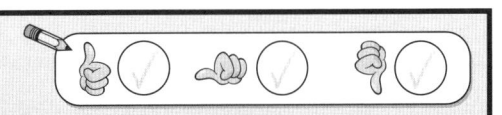

SECTION ONE — NUMBER AND PLACE VALUE

# Numbers on Scales

**1** What is the mass of the cake?

☐ g   ☐ 1 mark

**2** How tall is this duck?

☐ cm   ☐ 1 mark

**3** What length is shown on this ruler?

☐ cm   ☐ 1 mark

**4** Adam measures the temperature in his classroom.

What temperature does the thermometer show?

☐ °C   ☐ 1 mark

SECTION ONE — NUMBER AND PLACE VALUE

# Numbers on Scales

**5** Sarah is baking a cake. She needs 150 g of flour.

Draw an arrow pointing to 150 g on this scale.

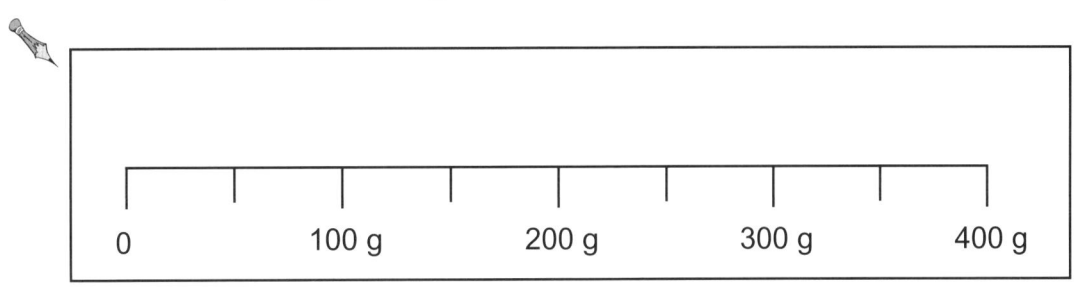

|  0    100 g    200 g    300 g    400 g |

*1 mark*

**6** Katie measures her height against a scale.

How tall is Katie?

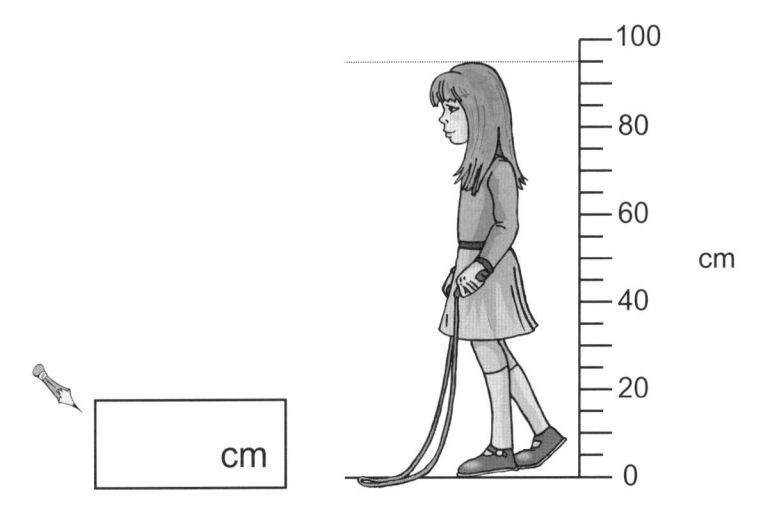

☐ cm

*1 mark*

**7** Look at this number line. Which numbers do the arrows point to?

Write the numbers in the boxes.

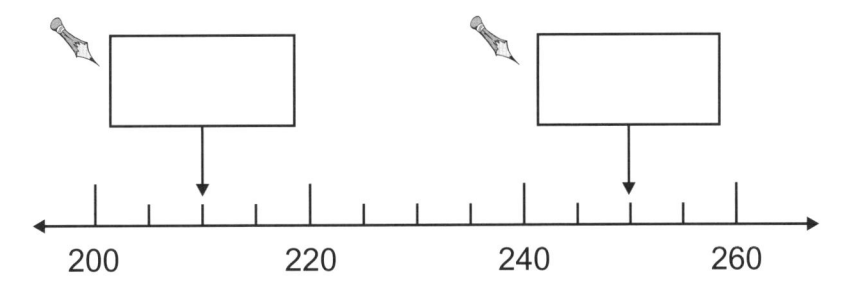

☐        ☐
↓        ↓
200   220   240   260

*2 marks*

"I can identify and estimate numbers on different number lines and scales."

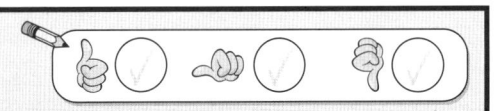

SECTION ONE — NUMBER AND PLACE VALUE

# Solving Number Problems

**1** A cafe sells 55 sandwiches on Monday and 32 on Tuesday.

How many did they sell altogether?

*1 mark*

**2** Gordon is playing rugby. He gets 4 points each time he scores.

Ken has 22 points. How many times must Gordon score to beat Ken?
Use the number line to help you.

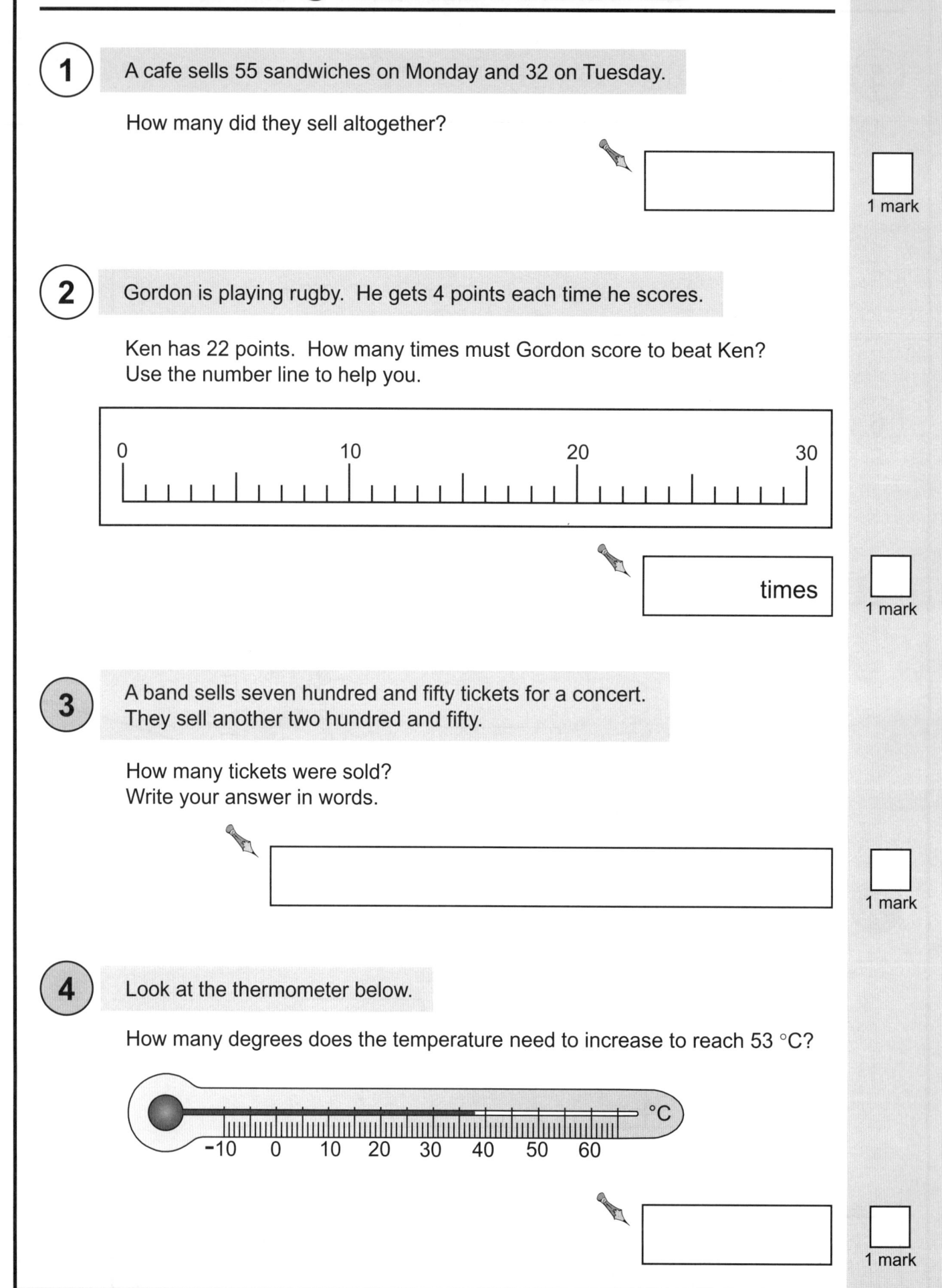

0    10    20    30

_____ times

*1 mark*

**3** A band sells seven hundred and fifty tickets for a concert.
They sell another two hundred and fifty.

How many tickets were sold?
Write your answer in words.

*1 mark*

**4** Look at the thermometer below.

How many degrees does the temperature need to increase to reach 53 °C?

*1 mark*

SECTION ONE — NUMBER AND PLACE VALUE

# Solving Number Problems

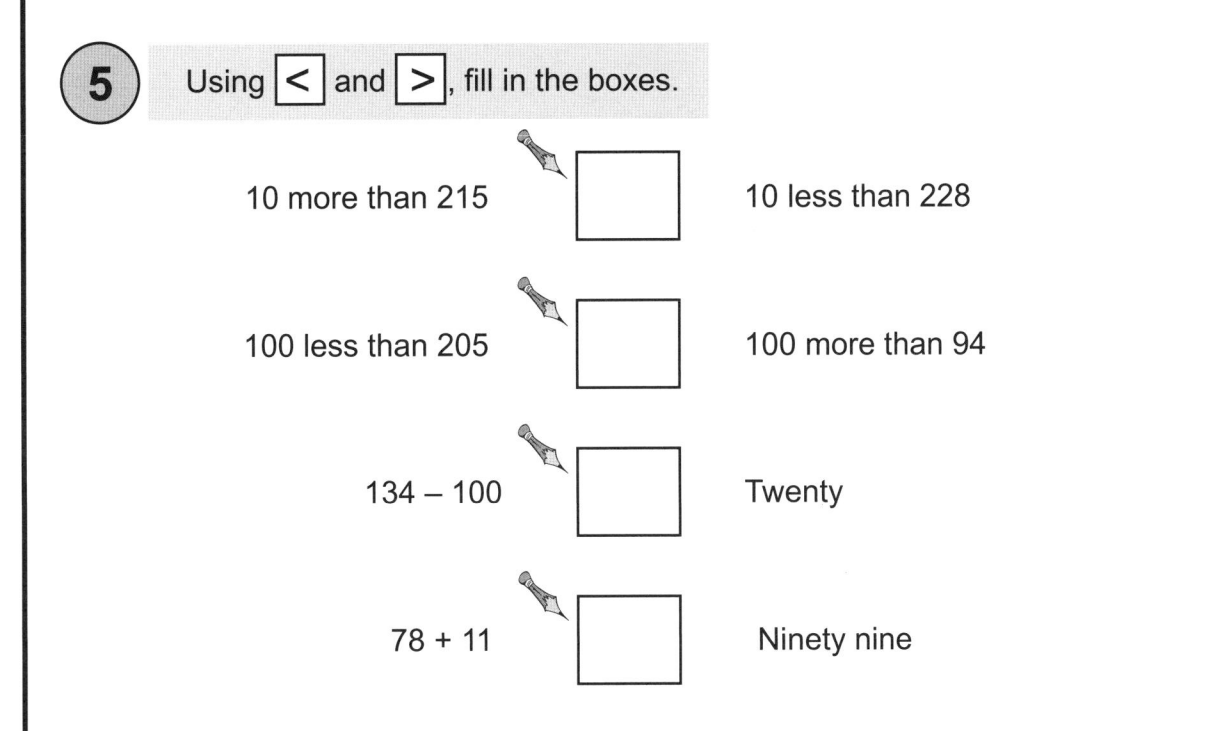

**5** Using < and >, fill in the boxes.

10 more than 215   ☐   10 less than 228

100 less than 205   ☐   100 more than 94

134 – 100   ☐   Twenty

78 + 11   ☐   Ninety nine

*2 marks*

**6** Emma is making cookies. She writes out her ingredients.

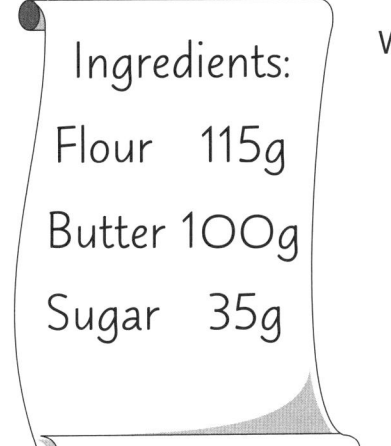

Ingredients:
Flour   115g
Butter  100g
Sugar   35g

What is the total mass of her ingredients?

☐ g

*1 mark*

Draw an arrow on the scale below to show your answer.

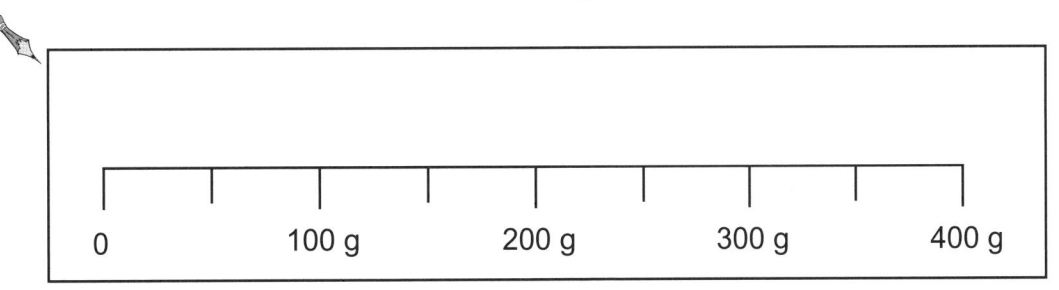

0 — 100 g — 200 g — 300 g — 400 g

*1 mark*

"I can solve problems using the things I've learnt about numbers."

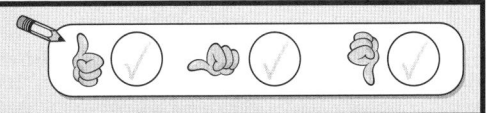

SECTION ONE — NUMBER AND PLACE VALUE

# Mental Addition

This page is on **mental** addition, so you need to do these sums in your head.

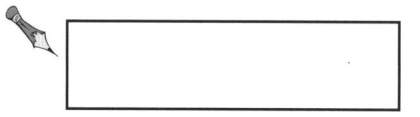

**1)** What is four hundred and fifty two plus forty?

1 mark

**2)** Calculate these sums.

324 + 4

241 + 500

716 + 70

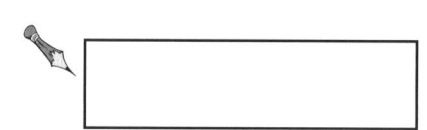

1 mark
1 mark
1 mark

**3)** Write a number in each box to make these sums correct.

120 + ☐ = 150

☐ + 200 = 240

☐ + 100 = 560

30 + ☐ = 170

2 marks

**4)** Draw circles around the three numbers that add up to 170.

20     30     50     60     80

1 mark

"I can add 1s, 10s and 100s to a 3-digit number."

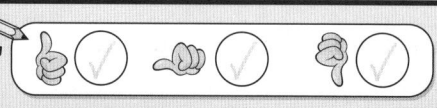

# Mental Subtraction

This page is on **mental** subtraction, so you need to do these calculations in your head.

**1)** Calculate:

158 – 5

160 – 40

295 – 50

563 – 200

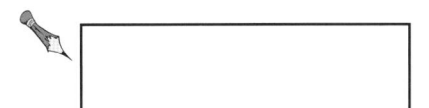

**2)** What is six hundred and eighty nine minus seventy?

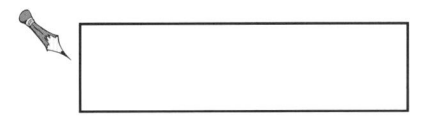

**3)** I subtract one number from another and get 90.

Circle the two numbers used.

150    220    290    340    430    510

**4)** What must I take away from 253 to make 173?

50    20    90    30    80    100

"I can subtract 1s, 10s and 100s from a 3-digit number."

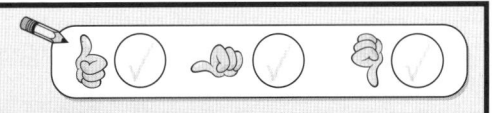

SECTION TWO — CALCULATIONS

# Written Addition

**1** Calculate 425 + 134.

[ ] 1 mark

**2** Ellen has £236. She is given £250. How much does she have now?

£ [ ] 1 mark

**3** What number is forty seven more than one hundred and eighty six?

[ ] 1 mark

**4** Georgina measures the heights of 2 sunflowers.

Flower A
Height: 79 cm

Flower B
Height: 128 cm

After 2 weeks, both flowers have grown 18 cm taller.
Calculate the heights of the sunflowers now.

Flower A [ ] cm    Flower B [ ] cm

2 marks

"I can add numbers with up to 3 digits using a written method."

SECTION TWO — CALCULATIONS

# **_Written Subtraction_**

**1** What is 688 − 51?

1 mark

**2** Calculate nine hundred and eighty one minus six hundred and seventy two.

1 mark

**3** Hannah has £115. Jake has £178.

How much more money than Hannah has Jake got?

£

1 mark

**4** Here are two buildings.

City Tower
Height: 381 metres

Town Hall
Height: 144 metres

How much taller is City Tower than Town Hall?   metres

1 mark

"I can subtract numbers with up to 3 digits using a written method."

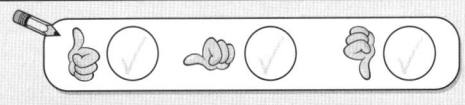

SECTION TWO — CALCULATIONS

# The 3, 4 and 8 Times Tables

**1** What is seven times eight?

1 mark

**2** Here is a list of numbers.

Circle all the numbers that are in the four times table.

24    10    32    16    14    26    8    20

1 mark

**3** Fill in the boxes to make these calculations correct:

5 × ☐ = 40          12 × 3 = ☐

2 marks

**4** Circle the numbers in this list that divide exactly by three.

18    29    11    21    15    7    25    36

1 mark

**5** Roland has 8 bags. He puts 3 cherries into each bag.

There is one cherry left over.
How many cherries did Roland start with?

☐ cherries

1 mark

"I know my tables for 3, 4 and 8 and their division facts."

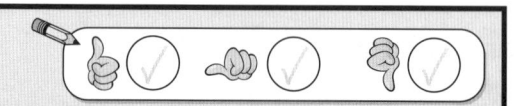

SECTION TWO — CALCULATIONS

# Using Times Tables Facts

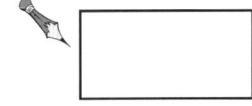

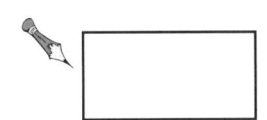

**1)** Work out the answers to these calculations:

4 × 5 × 2

5 × 8 × 4

4 × 8 × 3

**2)** Calculate:

8 × 60 =

eighty divided by two =

27 ÷ 3 =

**3)** What is 120 ÷ 3?

**4)** A farmer divides 45 sheep between 3 fields.

How many sheep are in each field?

_____ sheep

SECTION TWO — CALCULATIONS

# Using Times Tables Facts

**5** Calculate:

240 ÷ 4 =

300 ÷ 6 =

*2 marks*

**6** Work out:

34 × 4 =

25 × 8 =

49 × 3 =

*1 mark*
*1 mark*
*1 mark*

**7** What is two hundred and fifty six divided by four?

*1 mark*

**8** Lucy divides 144 sweets equally between 8 friends.

How many sweets does each friend get?

sweets

*1 mark*

"I can multiply and divide using my times tables and written methods."

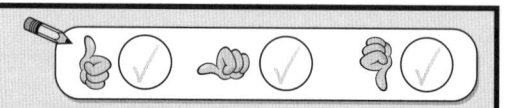

SECTION TWO — CALCULATIONS

# Estimating and Checking

**1)** Dan calculates that 43 − 17 = 26.

Write an inverse calculation he could use to check his answer.

☐

1 mark

**2)** Here are some divisions.

For each division, write a multiplication that uses the same numbers.

98 ÷ 2 = 49      ☐ × ☐ = ☐

1 mark

56 ÷ 7 = 8      ☐ × ☐ = ☐

1 mark

**3)** Holly wants to work out the answer to 48 + 29.

Write a simpler calculation Holly could use to estimate the answer.

☐

1 mark

Holly says, "48 plus 29 equals 87". Explain why Holly cannot be correct.

☐

1 mark

**4)** Ben divides 137 sweets equally between 9 bags.

Ben says, "There are 6 sweets in each bag".
Explain how you know that Ben is wrong without doing the calculation.

☐

1 mark

"I can estimate the answer to a calculation and use inverse operations to check answers."

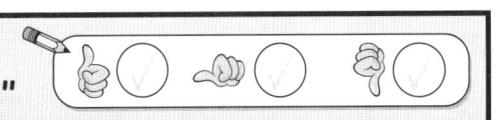

SECTION TWO — CALCULATIONS

# Solving Calculation Problems

**1)** 36 children split into 4 teams. Each team has the same number of children.

How many children are in each team?

[_____ children]

1 mark

**2)** A newspaper costs 80 pence.

Tom buys a newspaper every day.

How much will Tom spend on newspapers for:

four days?

[_____ pence]

1 mark

seven days?

[_____ pence]

1 mark

**3)** There are 5 classes in a school. There are 30 children in each class.

How many children are in the school?

[_____ children]

1 mark

**4)** Jane has 24 marbles. Rita has 4 times as many marbles as Jane.

How many marbles does Rita have?

[_____ marbles]

1 mark

Jane wins 17 more marbles. How many marbles does she have now?

[_____ marbles]

1 mark

SECTION TWO — CALCULATIONS

# Solving Calculation Problems

**5** Ryan is paid £4 a week to do a paper round.

Ryan wants to buy an mp3 player which costs £23.
How many weeks will he have to work for to be able to pay for it?

☐ weeks

1 mark

Ryan buys the mp3 player as soon as he has earned enough money.
How much money will he have left after he has bought the mp3 player?

£ ☐

1 mark

**6** Ben thinks of a number. He divides it by three and adds two.

He gets an answer of 9. What number was he thinking of?

☐

1 mark

**7** A cake has a mass of 520 g. It is cut into 8 equal slices.

What is the mass of 1 slice?

☐ g

1 mark

**8** Seeds are sold in 175 g bags.

How many grams of seeds are in three bags?

☐ g

1 mark

"I can solve problems by choosing the calculations I should do."

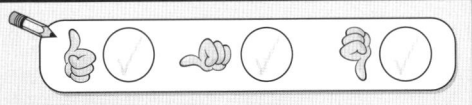

SECTION TWO — CALCULATIONS

# Counting in Tenths

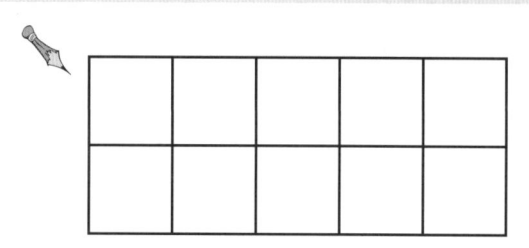

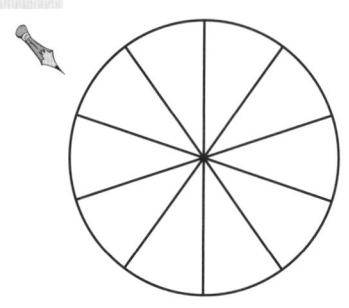

**1)** Shade $\frac{3}{10}$ of the rectangle and $\frac{7}{10}$ of the circle.

*2 marks*

**2)** Here is part of a number line. Write the letter of the arrow that points to $\frac{6}{10}$.

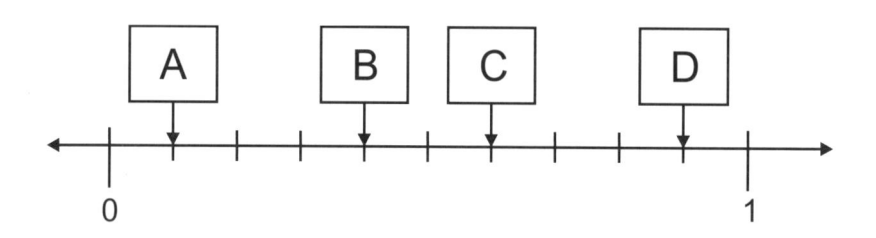

*1 mark*

**3)** What fraction of these shapes are squares?

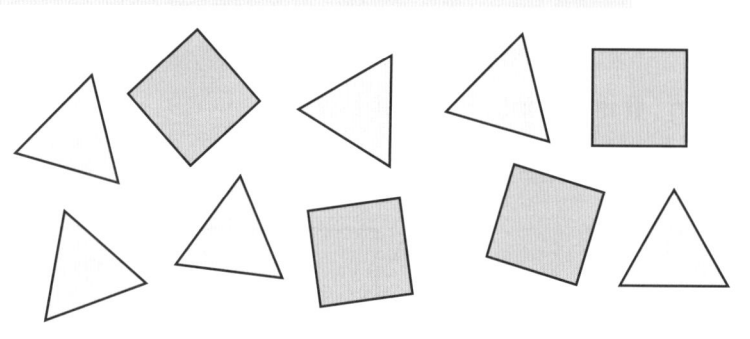

*1 mark*

**4)** Write the two missing fractions in the empty boxes.

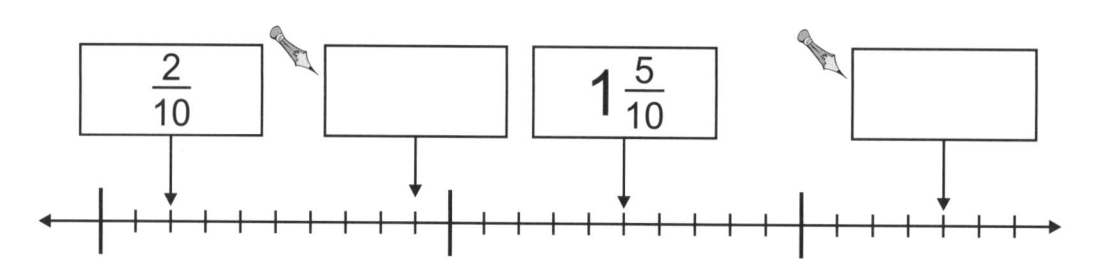

$\frac{2}{10}$ ⬜ $1\frac{5}{10}$ ⬜

*2 marks*

"I know that tenths come from dividing an object or number by 10. I can count up and down in tenths."

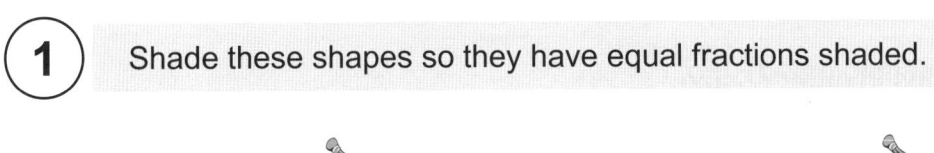

# Equivalent Fractions

**1)** Shade these shapes so they have equal fractions shaded.

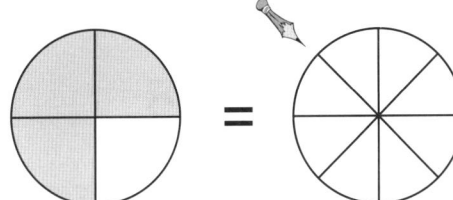

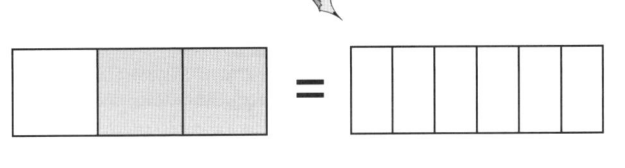

2 marks

**2)** $\frac{6}{8}$ of this shape is shaded. Write down a fraction equal to this.

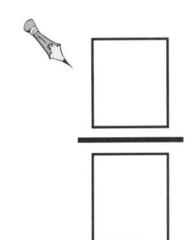

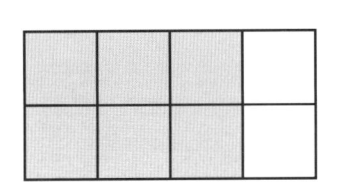

1 mark

**3)** Look at the shape below.

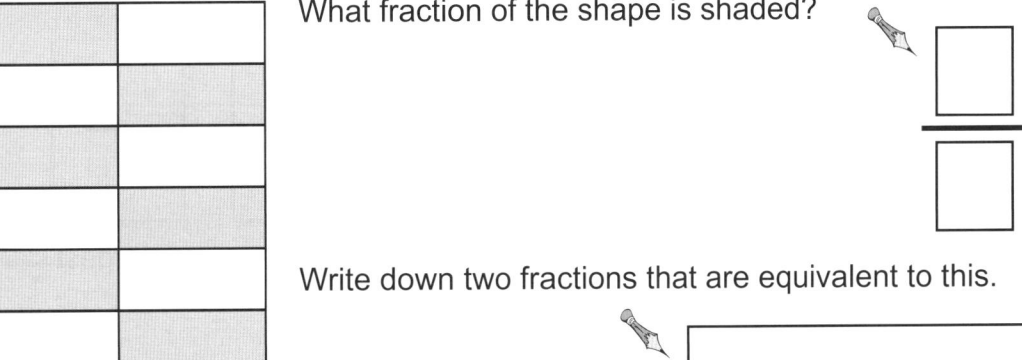

What fraction of the shape is shaded?

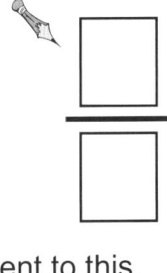

Write down two fractions that are equivalent to this.

2 marks

**4)** Circle the fraction below that is equal to one sixth.

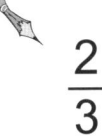

$\frac{2}{3}$  $\frac{6}{1}$  $\frac{1}{2}$  $\frac{2}{12}$

1 mark

"I can recognise and draw equivalent fractions."

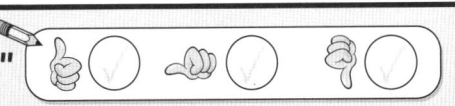

SECTION THREE — FRACTIONS

# Ordering Fractions

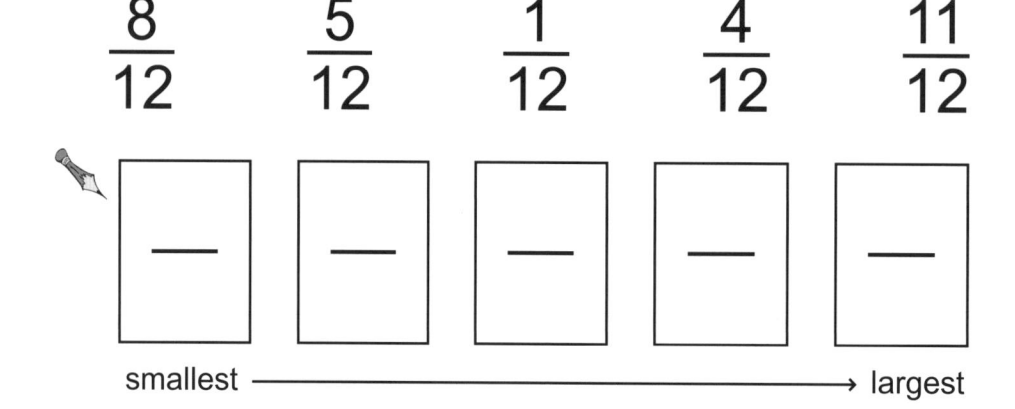

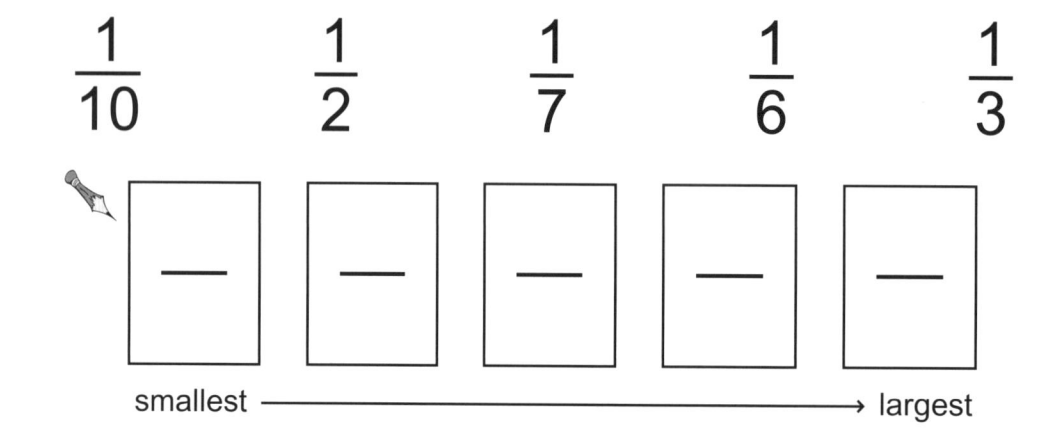

**1** Write these fractions in order of size.

$$\frac{8}{12} \quad \frac{5}{12} \quad \frac{1}{12} \quad \frac{4}{12} \quad \frac{11}{12}$$

smallest ⟶ largest

1 mark

**2** Write these fractions in order of size.

$$\frac{1}{10} \quad \frac{1}{2} \quad \frac{1}{7} \quad \frac{1}{6} \quad \frac{1}{3}$$

smallest ⟶ largest

1 mark

**3** Circle the smaller fraction in each pair.

$\frac{4}{12}$ or $\frac{6}{12}$ $\qquad$ $\frac{1}{2}$ or $\frac{1}{10}$

$\frac{1}{6}$ or $\frac{1}{5}$ $\qquad$ $\frac{1}{4}$ or $\frac{3}{4}$

2 marks

Section Three — Fractions

# Ordering Fractions

**4** Some children are trying to work out who won the most races at their school sports day.

They work out that:

Richard won $\frac{1}{9}$ of the races.

Matthew won $\frac{1}{5}$ of the races.

Bernard won $\frac{1}{10}$ of the races.

Who won the most races?

☐ 1 mark

**5** Here are some digit cards.

| 1 | 3 | 4 | 2 |

Use two of the cards to make:

a fraction which is less than $\frac{1}{3}$.

a fraction which is bigger than $\frac{1}{2}$.

☐ 2 marks

**6** Circle the bigger fraction.

$\frac{2}{6}$     $\frac{1}{4}$

☐ 1 mark

Explain how you know.

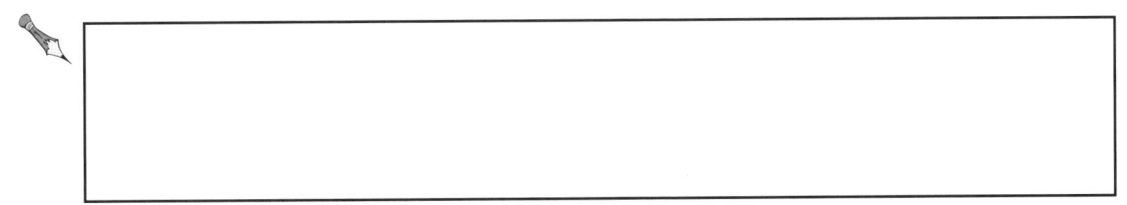

☐ 1 mark

"I can compare and order fractions by their size."

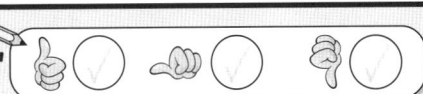

SECTION THREE — FRACTIONS

# Adding and Subtracting Fractions

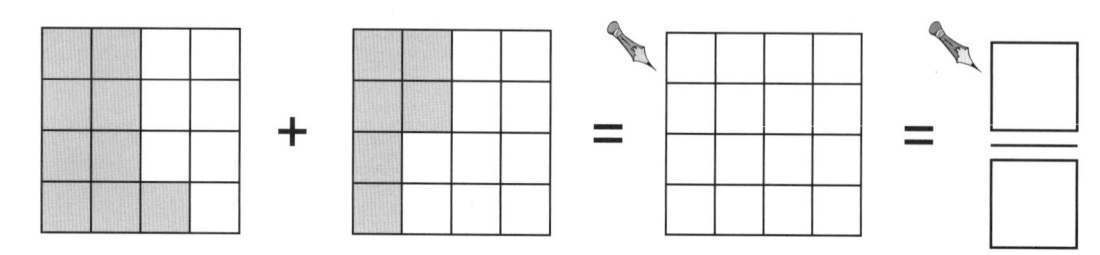

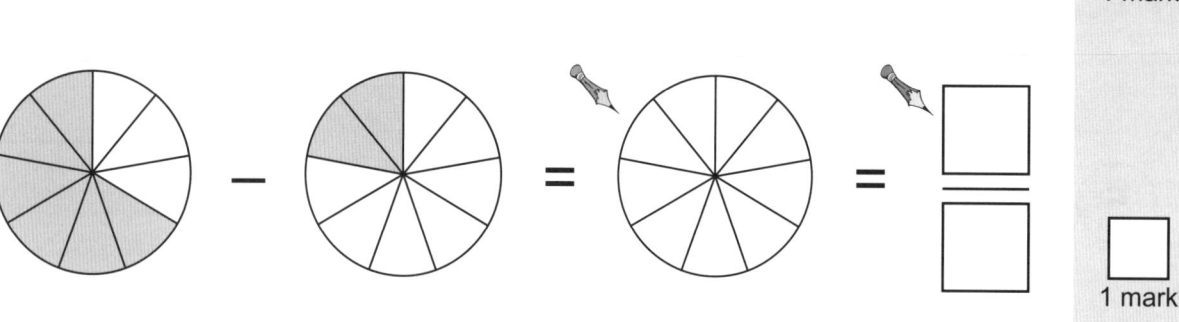

**1)** Shade in the last shape to show the answer and then write the answer as a fraction.

1 mark

1 mark

**2)** Calculate these sums.

$\frac{1}{5} + \frac{3}{5} = \frac{\square}{\square}$

$\frac{5}{10} + \frac{2}{10} = \frac{\square}{\square}$

$\frac{1}{3} + \frac{1}{3} = \frac{\square}{\square}$

$\frac{2}{8} + \frac{4}{8} = \frac{\square}{\square}$

4 marks

**3)** Find the answers to these calculations.

$\frac{5}{7} - \frac{2}{7} = \frac{\square}{\square}$

$\frac{9}{10} - \frac{4}{10} = \frac{\square}{\square}$

2 marks

SECTION THREE — FRACTIONS

# Adding and Subtracting Fractions

**4** What is seven ninths minus three ninths?

☐

1 mark

**5** Shayla ran $\frac{5}{15}$ of a mile on Monday and $\frac{9}{15}$ of a mile on Tuesday.

How far did she run in total?

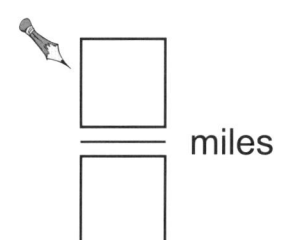

$\frac{\square}{\square}$ miles

1 mark

**6** Fill in the boxes to make the calculations correct.

$\frac{4}{\square} - \frac{\square}{10} = \frac{1}{10}$     $\frac{\square}{5} + \frac{1}{5} = \frac{3}{\square}$

2 marks

**7** Add these fractions together.

Shade in the fraction bar to help you.

$\frac{1}{6} + \frac{5}{12} = \frac{\square}{\square}$

1 mark

"I can add and subtract fractions with the same denominator."

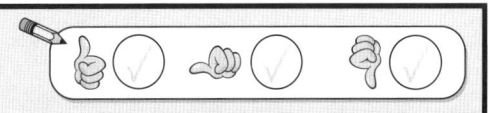

SECTION THREE — FRACTIONS

# Fractions of Amounts

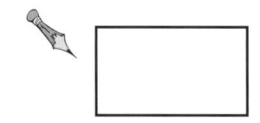

**1)** What is $\frac{1}{2}$ of 36? Circle the correct answer.

3    6    9    10    15    18    23

1 mark

**2)** What is $\frac{1}{4}$ of 24?

1 mark

**3)** Sophie has 12 pet snails. $\frac{1}{3}$ of them have blue shells.

How many snails have blue shells?

snails

1 mark

**4)** Amir has 16 squares of chocolate. He eats $\frac{3}{8}$ of the chocolate.

How many squares of chocolate does Amir eat? Use the picture to help you.

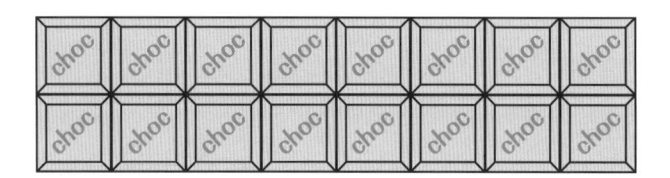

squares

1 mark

**5)** Steve has a bag of 20 sweets. Three quarters are green.

How many sweets are green?

sweets

1 mark

SECTION THREE — FRACTIONS

# Fractions of Amounts

**6** Mark has 40 marbles. He gives $\frac{1}{10}$ of them away.

How many marbles does he have left?

_____ marbles

1 mark

**7** What is $\frac{5}{8}$ of 56? Circle the correct answer.

12     34     10     29     35     17     41

1 mark

**8** Work out:

three quarters of 40

1 mark

two thirds of 9

1 mark

four fifths of 30

1 mark

**9** Gary the mole's total height is 30 cm.

$\frac{2}{5}$ of Gary the mole is above ground.
How much of Gary is above ground?
Give your answer in cm.

_____ cm

1 mark

"I can find a fraction of an amount, such as two fifths of 10."

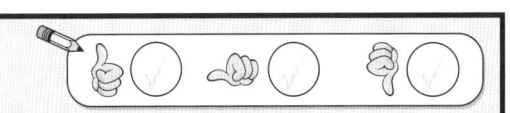

SECTION THREE — FRACTIONS

# Solving Fraction Problems

**1)** Pete drinks 9 cups of tea every day. 4 of those cups of tea are green.

Write how many cups of green tea he drinks as a fraction.

**2)** Mia is reading a book. She has read $\frac{4}{10}$ so far.

How many tenths of the book does Mia have left to read?

**3)** Zak has saved £12. He spends a quarter of his money on a book and one third on a pen.

How much does the book cost?

How much does the pen cost?

**4)** Two fifths of Chloe's hair is blue. What fraction of her hair is not blue?

**5)** Chris has 32 kg of sprouts. He gives $\frac{3}{8}$ of them to Linda.

How many sprouts does he have left?

kg

SECTION THREE — FRACTIONS

# Solving Fraction Problems

**6** Four children eat $\frac{2}{9}$ of a chocolate cake each.

What fraction of the cake do they eat in total?

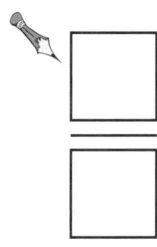

☐/☐

1 mark

**7** Fill in the boxes.

one half of ☐ is 9.

1 mark

one third of ☐ is 10.

1 mark

☐ of 12 is 3.

1 mark

**8** Amir eats $\frac{1}{3}$ of a pizza and Jo eats $\frac{1}{6}$ of it.

What fraction of the pizza is left?

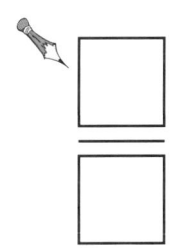

☐/☐

1 mark

**9** Write in the missing numbers.

$\frac{1}{2}$ of ☐ = $\frac{1}{4}$ of 24

1 mark

"I can solve problems that involve fractions."

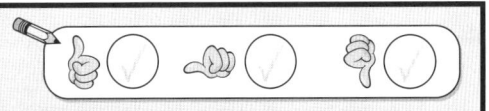

SECTION THREE — FRACTIONS

# Length, Mass and Volume

**1** These lengths are written in centimetres. Change them into millimetres.

Write your answers in the boxes.

3 cm = [ ] mm        5 cm = [ ] mm

**2** Change these units of measurement.

3 litres into millilitres.        200 cm into metres.

[ ] ml        [ ] m

**3** Which of these two lengths is longer? Circle the correct answer.

2100 mm        220 cm

**4** Henry buys two sandwiches of different masses.

Sandwich 1 has a mass of 524 g.
Sandwich 2 has a mass of 476 g.

Work out the total mass of the two sandwiches in kilograms.

[ ] kg

**5** Jim has some metal shapes. Each shape has a mass of 100 g.

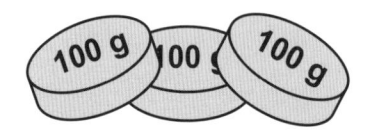

Jim makes a pile of the shapes. The pile has a mass of 2 kg.
How many shapes are in the pile?

[ ] shapes

# Length, Mass and Volume

**6** How long is this crayon in mm? The diagram is not drawn actual size.

[ ] mm

**7** The diagram shows water in a container.

Josh pours 250 ml of the water away.
How much water is left in the container?

[ ] ml

**8** Saba has some square tiles. Each tile has a width of 50 cm.

Saba lays the tiles side by side in a line.
How many tiles will she need to make a line 2 m long?

[ ] tiles

**9** A carton holds 2 litres of apple juice.

Emily fills 12 glasses with apple juice. She puts 100 ml in each glass.
How much apple juice is left in the carton? Give your answer in millilitres.
Show your working.

[ ] ml

"I can compare, add and subtract lengths, masses and volumes."

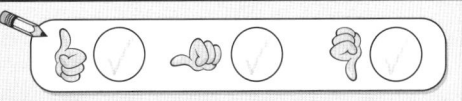

SECTION FOUR — MEASUREMENT

# Perimeter

**1)** Claire's garden is a rectangle.

Work out its perimeter.

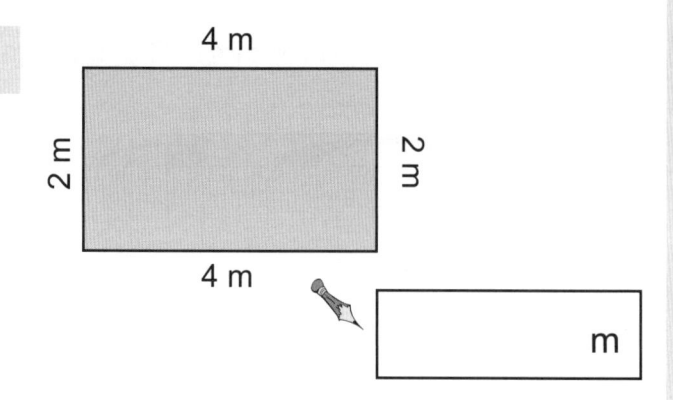

4 m, 2 m, 2 m, 4 m

_____ m

1 mark

**2)** Look at the triangle to the right.

Work out its perimeter.

3 cm, 3 cm, 4 cm

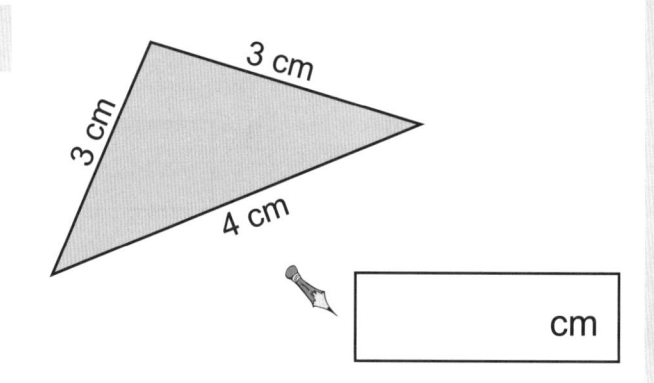

_____ cm

1 mark

**3)** A shape has sides of length 2 cm, 3 cm, 5 cm, 1 cm, and 4 cm.

Work out its perimeter.

_____ cm

1 mark

**4)** Look at the shape to the right.

Work out its perimeter.

2 mm, 1 mm, 2 mm, 1 mm, 2 mm

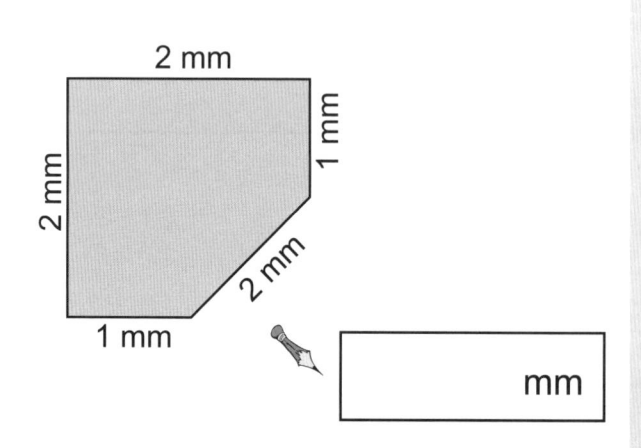

_____ mm

1 mark

SECTION FOUR — MEASUREMENT

# Perimeter

**5** Here is a centimetre square grid.

Draw a rectangle with a perimeter of 16 cm.

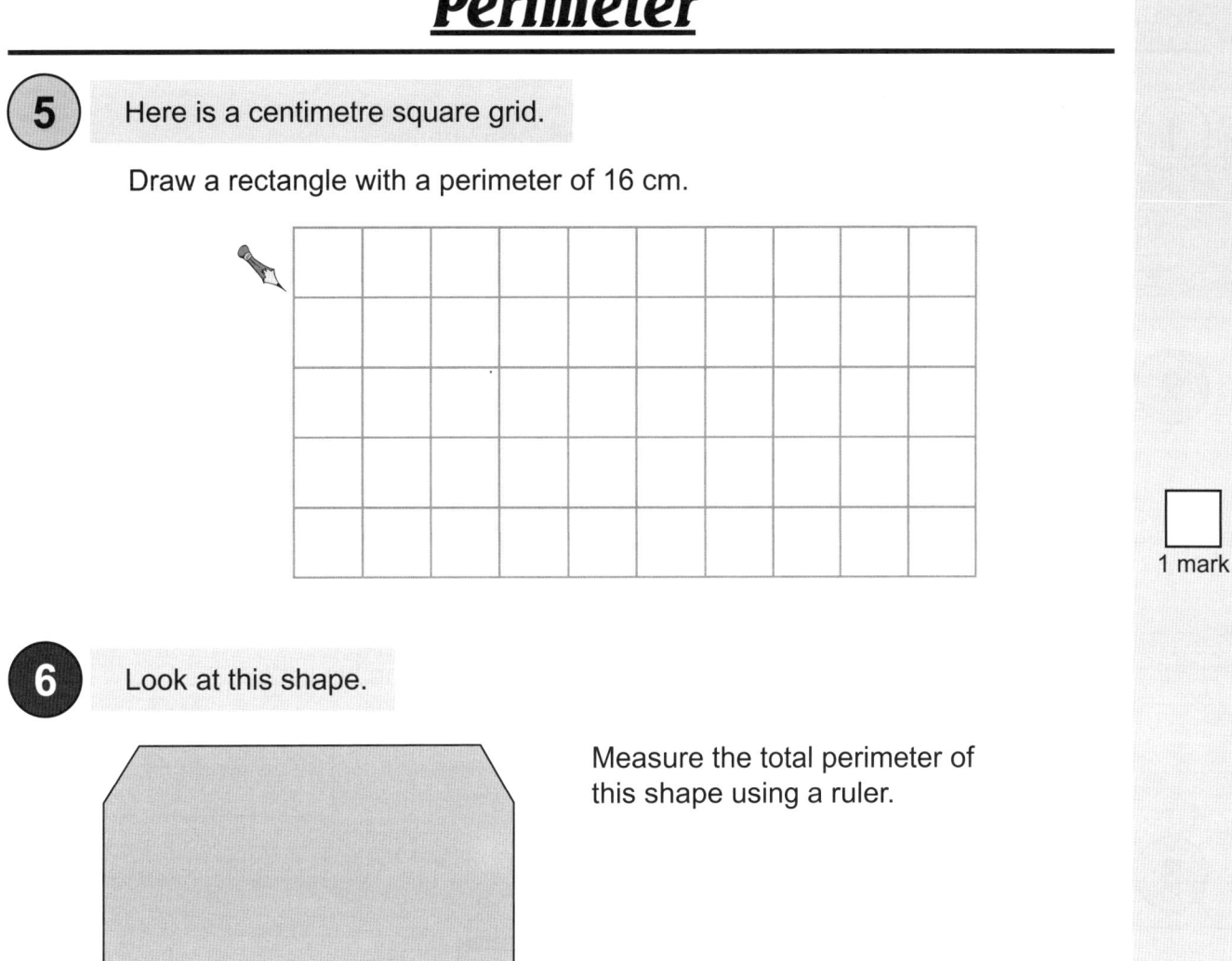

1 mark

**6** Look at this shape.

Measure the total perimeter of this shape using a ruler.

☐ cm

1 mark

**7** Leona makes a shape using equilateral triangles.

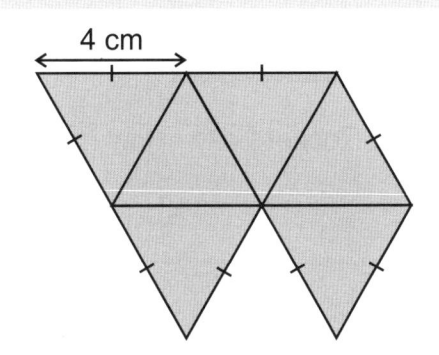

4 cm

Not actual size

Each side of a triangle is 4 cm long. What is the perimeter of the shape?

☐ cm

1 mark

"I can measure the perimeter of a 2D shape."

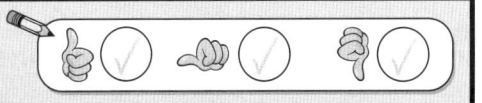

SECTION FOUR — MEASUREMENT

# Money

**1** Simon has 95 pence. He buys a bread roll for 53 pence.

How much money does he have left?

____ p

**2** Hasan has £3. He has been given a shopping list.

Socks    £1.20
Potatoes 85p
Beans    75p

How much do the items cost altogether?

£ ____

Does he have enough money to buy everything on his list?

____

**3** Here is the price list for an ice cream van.

*Price List*

Rocket Lolly    £1.27

Fruit Crush     £1.45

Choc Surprise   £2.05

Harriet buys a Choc Surprise and a Rocket Lolly. How much does she pay?

£ ____

John buys a Fruit Crush with a £2 coin. How much change does he get?

____ p

"I can add and subtract money to give change."

SECTION FOUR — MEASUREMENT

# Clocks

**1)** Draw lines to match each clock to the correct time.

a)   b)   c)   d)

6:07         4:50         11:33
      5:08         8:23

2 marks

**2)** Write these times in words.

[analogue clock]            [19:20]

_____            _____

2 marks

**3)** Laura finishes a race in 2 minutes.

How many seconds is this?          _____ seconds

1 mark

**4)** How many days are in:

January? _____            September? _____

A leap year? _____            February in a normal year? _____

2 marks

"I can tell the time from 12 and 24 hour clocks.
I know how days are sorted into months and years."

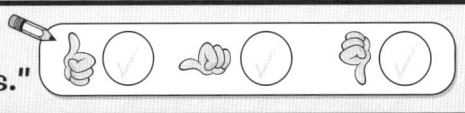

*Section Four — Measurement*

# Time Problems

**1)** Alan goes to sleep at 9 o'clock at night. He wakes up nine hours later.

What time does Alan wake up? Write am or pm in your answer.

[ ]  1 mark

**2)** Trains take 1 hour and 30 minutes to travel from London to Bristol.

This timetable shows the times of some trains.
Fill in the gaps in the timetable.

| Leaves from London | 1:00 |      | 3:20 |
| --- | --- | --- | --- |
| Arrives in Bristol | 2:30 | 3:50 |      |

2 marks

**3)** Here is a bus timetable.

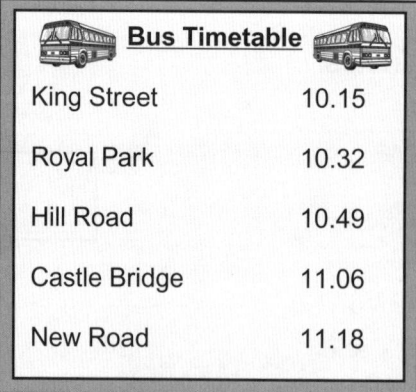

**Bus Timetable**

| King Street | 10.15 |
| --- | --- |
| Royal Park | 10.32 |
| Hill Road | 10.49 |
| Castle Bridge | 11.06 |
| New Road | 11.18 |

Mark gets on the bus at King Street. He gets off at Castle Bridge.
How long does his journey last?

[ ] minutes   1 mark

Hannah arrives at Hill Road bus stop at 10.23.
How long will she have to wait for the bus?

[ ] minutes   1 mark

SECTION FOUR — MEASUREMENT

# Time Problems

**4** Andrew walks to the park in the afternoon.

This is the time on the clock when he leaves the house:

This is the time on his watch when he arrives at the park:

How long does it take Andrew to walk to the park?

............ minutes  □ 1 mark

**5** This sign shows the opening times for a shop during the week.

**OPENING TIMES**

| Monday | 9:00 am — 5:30 pm |
| Tuesday | 9:00 am — 5:30 pm |
| Wednesday | 9:00 am — 1:00 pm |
| Thursday | 9:00 am — 5:30 pm |
| Friday | 1:30 pm — 6:00 pm |

For how long is the shop open on a Monday?

............ hours  □ 1 mark

Which day has the shortest opening time?

............  □ 1 mark

Lauren arrives at the shop at 12:55 pm on a Friday.
How long does she have to wait until the shop opens?

............ minutes  □ 1 mark

*"I can compare different lengths of time.
I can work out how long an activity takes
and when an event starts or finishes."*

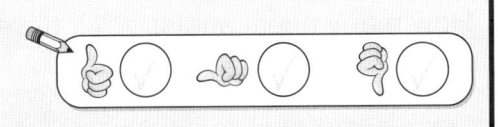

SECTION FOUR — MEASUREMENT

# 2D Shapes

**1.** Draw lines to match each shape with its name. The first one has been done for you.

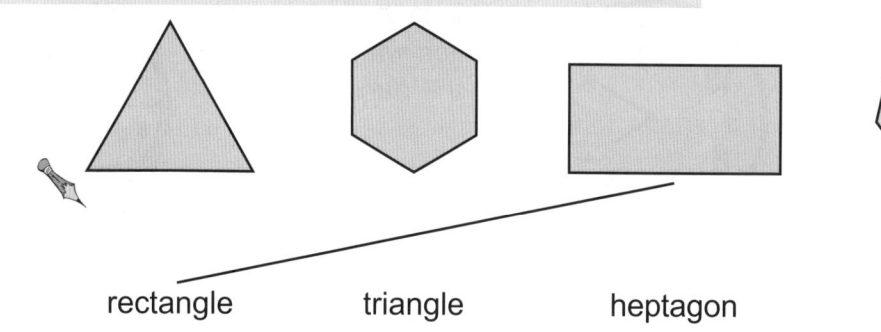

rectangle     triangle     heptagon     hexagon

**2.** Here is part of a shape.
Draw more straight lines to make it into a pentagon.

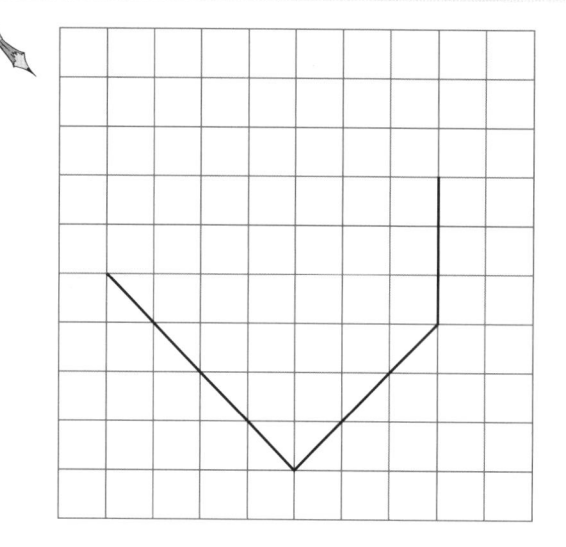

**3.** Ken draws some shapes.

Circle the quadrilaterals.

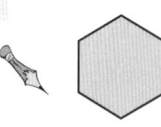

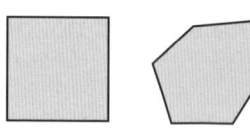

**4.** Tom draws an equilateral triangle.

How many equal sides will it have?

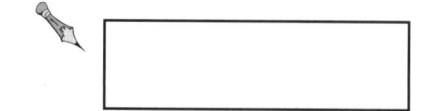

How many equal angles will it have?

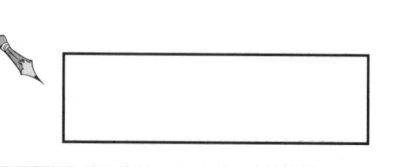

# 2D Shapes

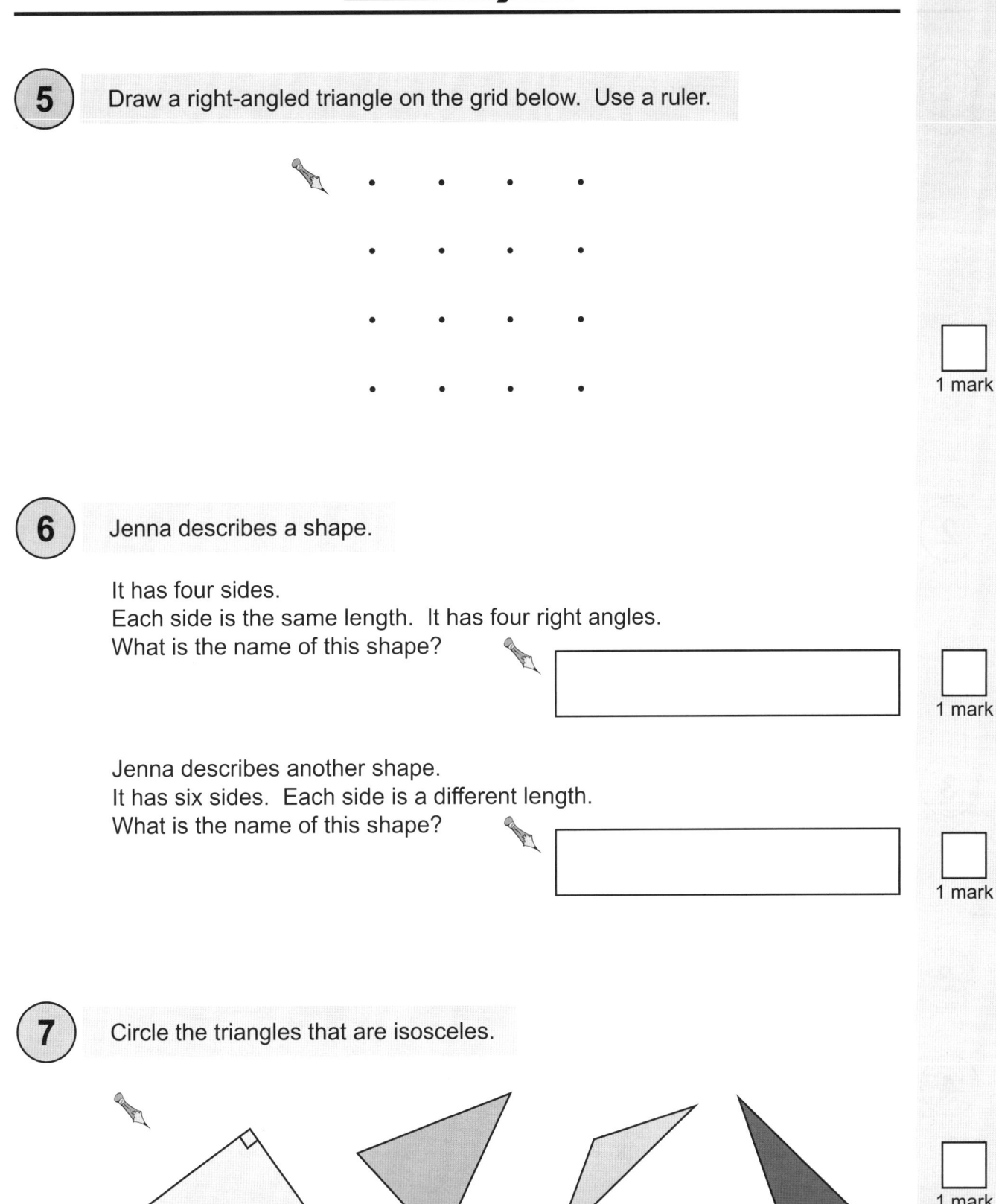

**5** Draw a right-angled triangle on the grid below. Use a ruler.

1 mark

**6** Jenna describes a shape.

It has four sides.
Each side is the same length. It has four right angles.
What is the name of this shape?

1 mark

Jenna describes another shape.
It has six sides. Each side is a different length.
What is the name of this shape?

1 mark

**7** Circle the triangles that are isosceles.

1 mark

"I can draw and describe 2D shapes."

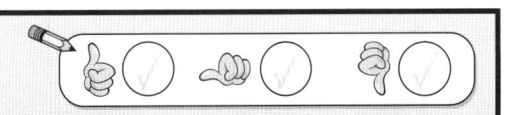

SECTION FIVE — GEOMETRY

# 3D Shapes

**1)** Name each 3D shape below.

[cube]

[sphere]

[cone]

1 mark

**2)** Circle the shapes that are prisms.

1 mark

**3)** Draw lines to match these 3D shapes to their properties.

sphere                each face is a triangle

tetrahedron           no flat surfaces

cube                  has six faces

1 mark

**4)** How many faces does each shape have?

Write the correct number in each box.

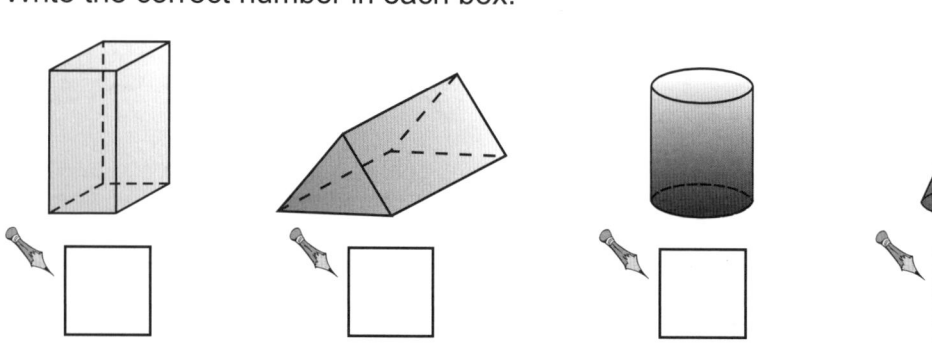

1 mark

SECTION FIVE — GEOMETRY

# 3D Shapes

**5** Jack makes a square-based pyramid out of sticks and balls of clay.

How many sticks does he use?

_____ sticks  [1 mark]

How many balls of clay does he use?

_____ balls of clay  [1 mark]

**6** How many edges does a tetrahedron have?

_____ edges  [1 mark]

**7** Dave is thinking of a solid shape.

It has one curved face.
It has two other faces that are circles.
What is the name of this shape?

_____  [1 mark]

Dave thinks of another solid shape.
It has 6 rectangular faces.
Not all of the sides are identical.
What shape is Dave thinking of?

_____  [1 mark]

"I can recognise and describe 3D shapes."

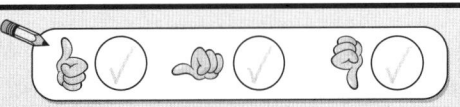

SECTION FIVE — GEOMETRY

# Angles and Lines

**1** Circle any right angles on the shapes below.
Use a set square to help you.

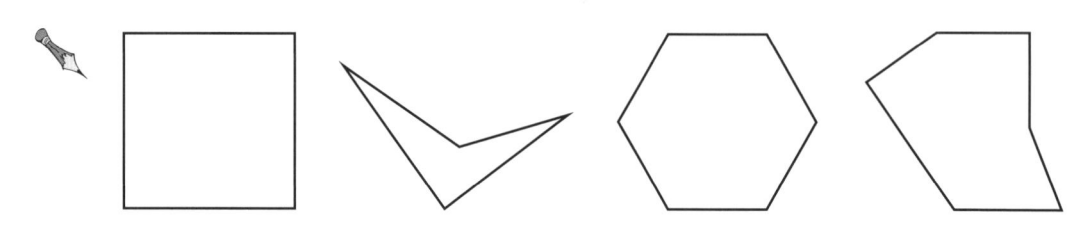

1 mark

**2** A spinning top spins one full turn.

How many quarter turns has it done?

1 mark

**3** An obtuse angle is an angle larger than a right angle.
Circle all the obtuse angles below.

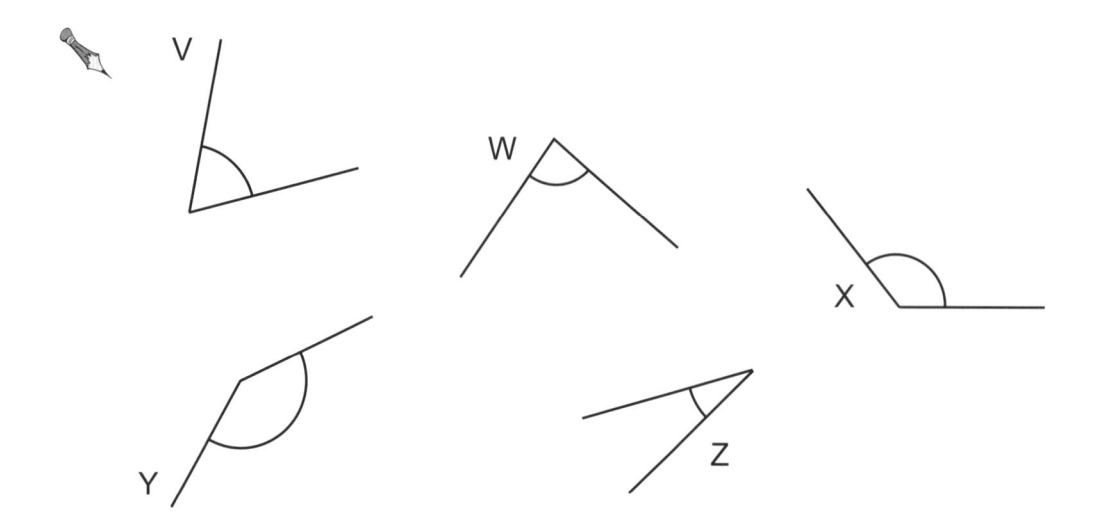

V    W    X    Y    Z

1 mark

"I know what a right angle is and how many right angles are in a ¼, ½, ¾ and full turn."

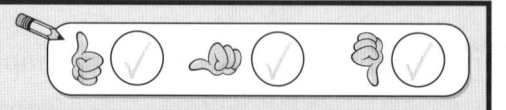

# Angles and Lines

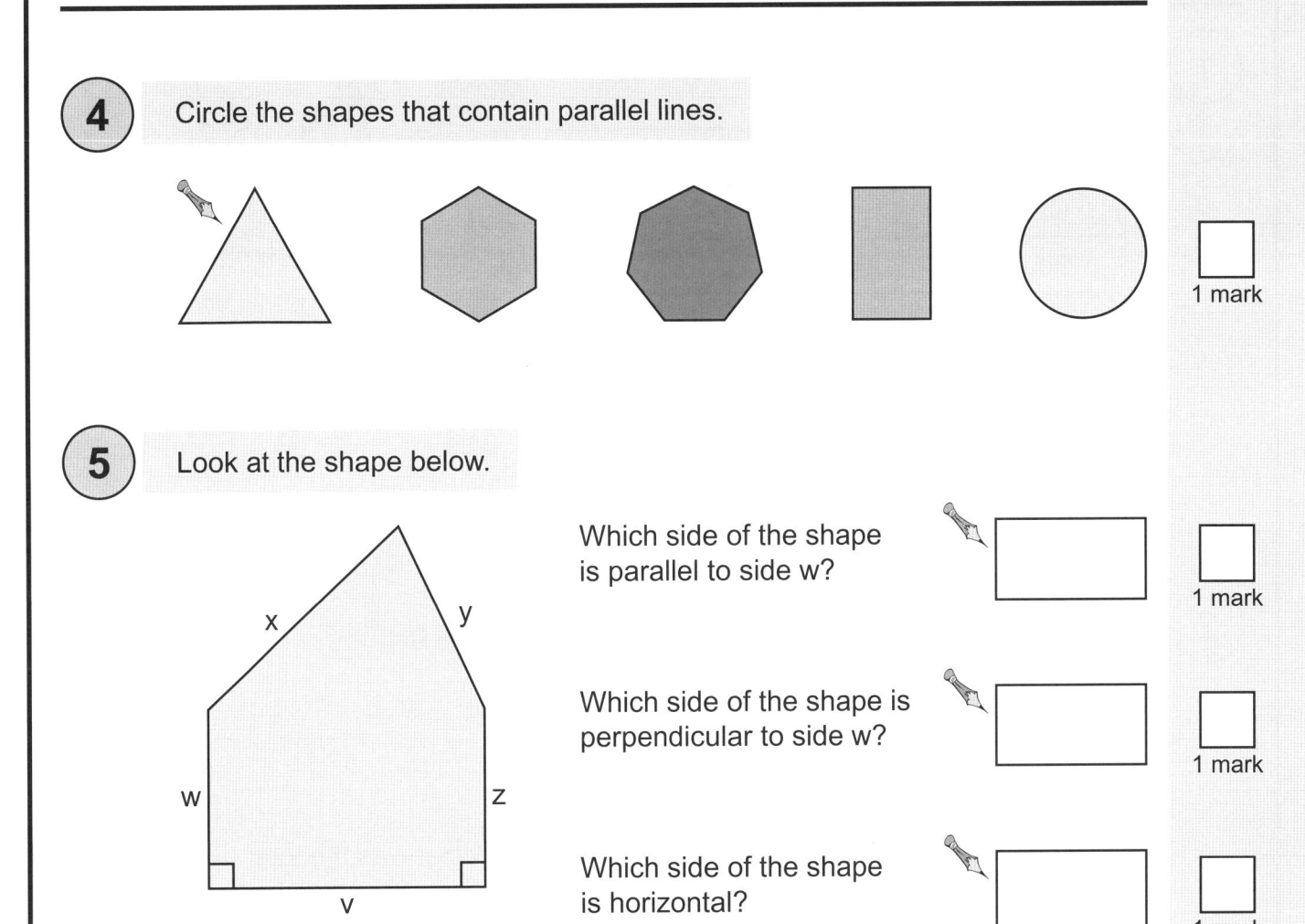

**4** Circle the shapes that contain parallel lines.

1 mark

**5** Look at the shape below.

Which side of the shape is parallel to side w?

1 mark

Which side of the shape is perpendicular to side w?

1 mark

Which side of the shape is horizontal?

1 mark

**6** Draw two more lines on the grid to make a shape with two pairs of parallel sides.

Use a ruler.

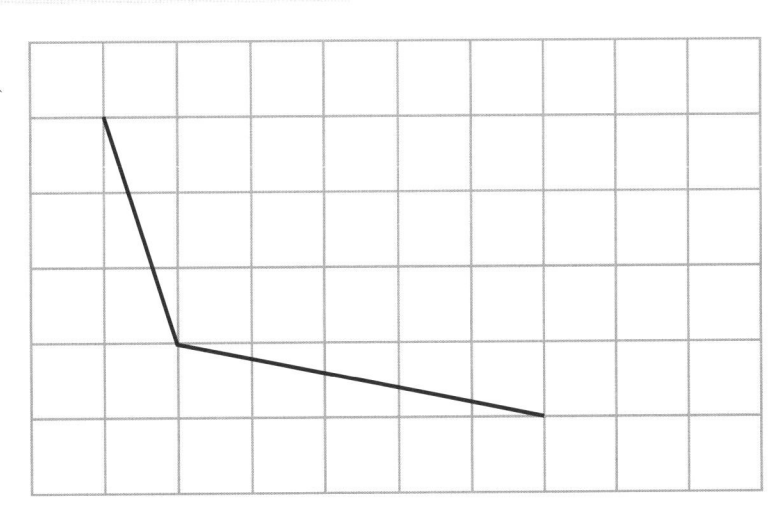

1 mark

"I can identify horizontal, vertical, parallel and perpendicular lines."

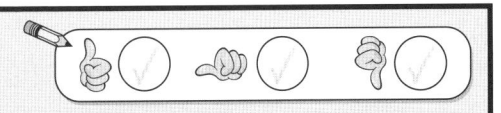

SECTION FIVE — GEOMETRY

# Tables

**1** Use the picture to complete the tally chart.

| Animal | Tally | Frequency |
|---|---|---|
| Cat | | |
| Dog | | |
| Rabbit | | |

How many more dogs are there than rabbits?

**2** Harry counted the numbers of different birds in his back garden.

Complete Harry's table.

| Bird | Tally | Frequency |
|---|---|---|
| blackbird | | 6 |
| crow | ℍℍ |||| | 9 |
| sparrow | |||| | |
| starling | ℍℍ ℍℍ ℍℍ | | |

What was the total number of birds?

_____ birds

**3** Rachel records the colours of the cars that pass her school.

Here are her results.

blue  red  blue  silver  red  blue  silver  red  blue  red
red  red  blue  silver  red  silver  blue  blue  silver  red

Construct and label a tally chart to present this information.

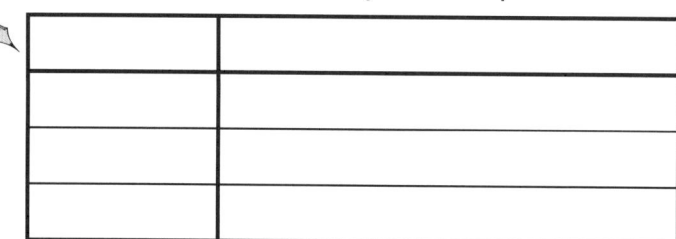

"I can interpret and present data using tables."

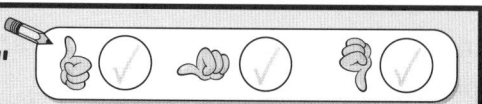

# Bar Charts

**1** This table shows the numbers of different fish that Emma sold.

Use this table to complete the bar chart.

| Fish | Number sold |
|---|---|
| Cod | 20 |
| Haddock | 14 |
| Plaice | 9 |
| Skate | 16 |

What was the total number of fish that Emma sold?

☐ fish

**Bar chart to show the numbers of different fish that Emma sold**

1 mark

1 mark

**2** Ed sells four flavours of crisps at his café.

He records the number of each flavour he sold in a bar chart.

**Bar chart to show the numbers of different flavour crisps sold on Saturday**

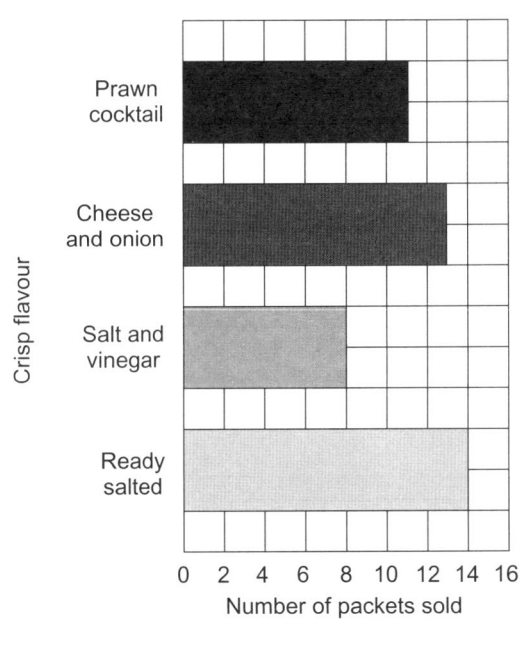

What was the most popular flavour?

☐

1 mark

How many packets of prawn cocktail flavour crisps did Ed sell?

☐ packets

1 mark

How many packets of crisps did Ed sell in total?

☐ packets

1 mark

"I can interpret and present data using bar charts."

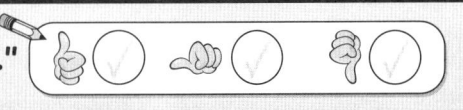

SECTION SIX — STATISTICS

# Pictograms

**1** Noah counted the different birds he spotted at the park.

He put his data into a table.

| Type of bird | Number of birds |
|---|---|
| Duck | 11 |
| Goose | 6 |
| Pigeon | 14 |
| Swan | 5 |

Use the data from the table to complete the pictogram.

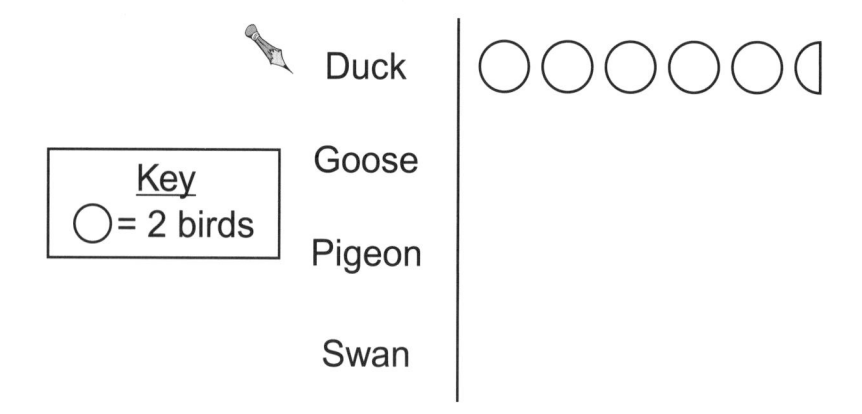

Duck ⭕⭕⭕⭕⭕◗

Key
◯ = 2 birds

Goose

Pigeon

Swan

2 marks

Noah added 4½ circles to the pictogram to show how many starlings he saw.
How many starlings did he see?

_____ starlings

1 mark

Theo says he spotted 17 pigeons at the park.
How many circles would this be on the pictogram?

_____ circles

1 mark

"I can interpret and present data using pictograms."

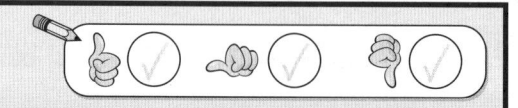

SECTION SIX — STATISTICS

# Interpreting Tables and Charts

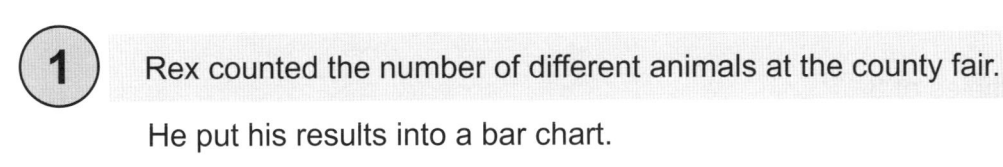

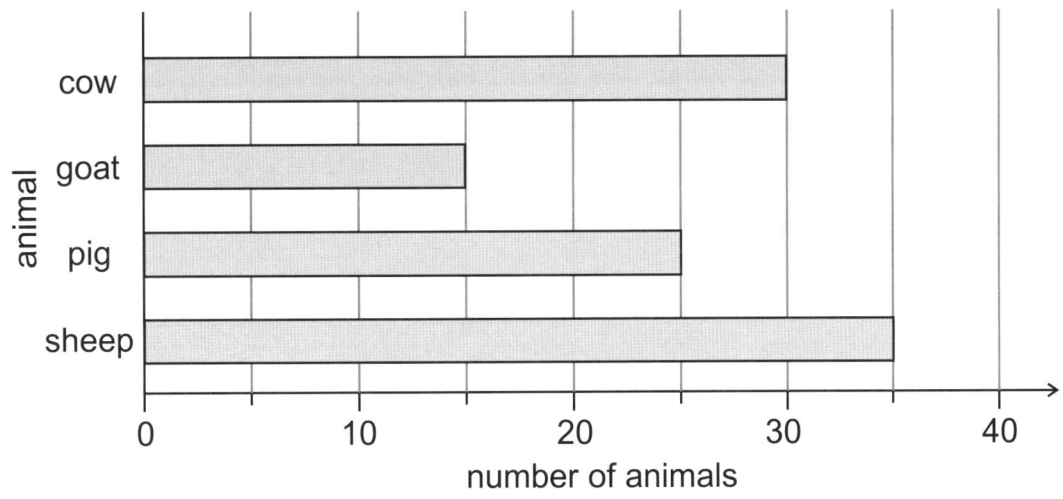

**1** Rex counted the number of different animals at the county fair.

He put his results into a bar chart.

How many pigs were there? ☐ pigs

How many more sheep than goats were there? ☐

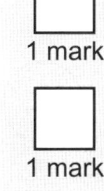

**2** The pictogram shows the number of girls in different years in a school.

Key ◯ = 4 girls

How many girls are there altogether in years 3, 4, 5 and 6?

☐ girls

How many fewer girls are in Year 4 than Year 6?

☐ girls

"I can answer questions using information from tables, bar charts and pictograms."

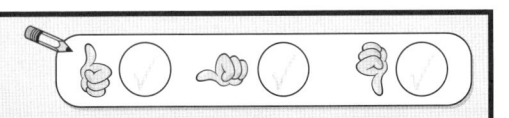

*Section Six — Statistics*

# Year Three Objectives Test

**1)** Circle the multiples of 8.

24      28      65      32      48

1 mark

**2)** Find $\frac{1}{3}$ of 36.

1 mark

**3)** Circle the right angles.

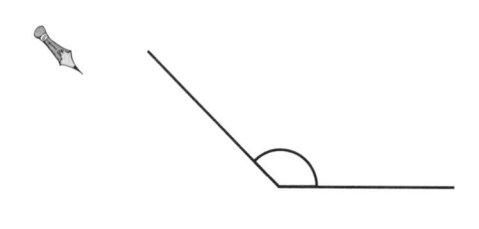

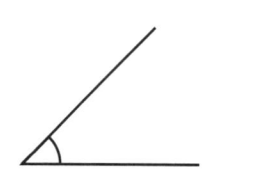

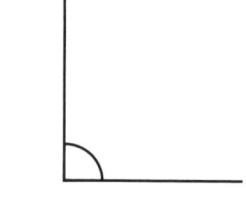

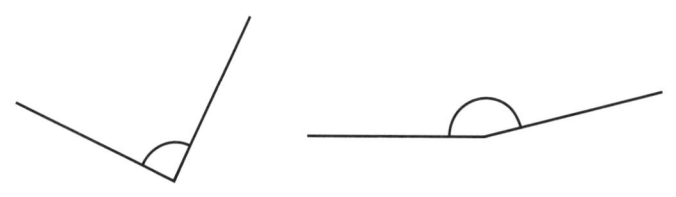

2 marks

**4)** Each calculation on the number balance has the same answer. Write in the missing number.

3 × 4          20 − ☐

1 mark

**5** Write in the missing digits.

$$54 \div \boxed{\phantom{0}} = 6$$

$$54 - 3\boxed{\phantom{0}} = 18$$

**6** Four teams played in a football competition.
The pictogram shows how many goals were scored by each team.

Team A | ◯ ◖
Team B | ◯ ◯ ◯ ◯
Team C | ◯ ◯ ◖
Team D | ◯ ◯ ◯

◯ = 2 goals

How many goals did Team A score? ☐ goals

How many more goals did Team B score than Team C? ☐ goals

**7** Calculate 178 – 87.

**8** Calculate 13 × 4.

[ ] 1 mark

**9** Imran started to run at 7:35 am.
He stopped running at 8:15 am.

How long did he run for?

[ ] minutes   1 mark

**10** Circle the shape that has exactly one pair of parallel sides.

A   B   C   D   E

1 mark

**11** Draw a line to match each clock face to the same time on a digital clock.

1:50

2:55

11:20

5:45

7:50

2 marks

**12** Shade the grid on the right so that the same fraction is shaded as the grid on the left.

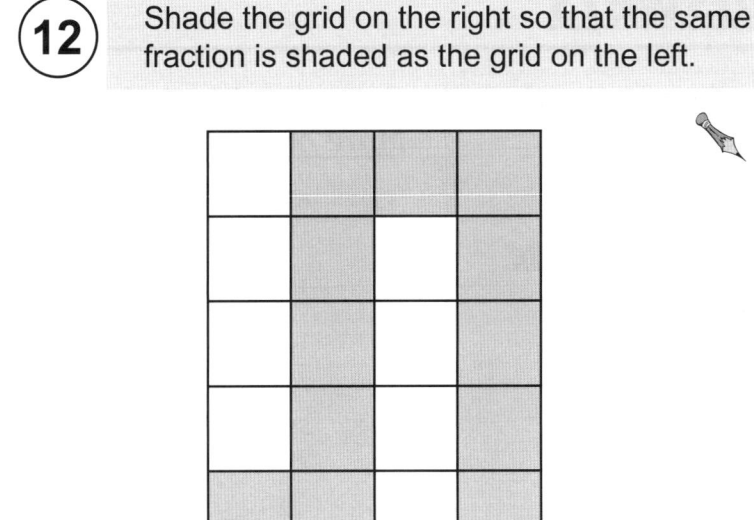

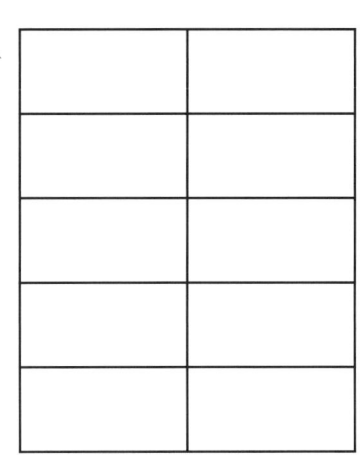

*1 mark*

**13** Write the missing number to make this correct.

$$\frac{1}{3} \text{ of } 33 = \frac{1}{2} \text{ of } \boxed{\phantom{00}}$$

*1 mark*

**14** Karl has £5. He buys a book for £3.85. How much money does he have left?

£ ☐

*1 mark*

**15** Use the signs =, < or > to make these correct.

3 × 3  ☐  2 × 4

6 × 4  ☐  8 × 3

5 × 4  ☐  7 × 3

*2 marks*

YEAR THREE OBJECTIVES TEST

# Answers

## Pages 2-5 — Year Two Objectives Test

Q1 **12** *(1 mark)*

Q2 **4 tens** or **40** *(1 mark)*

Q3 **eighty nine** *(1 mark)*

Q4 *(1 mark)*

Q5 **15, 18, 21** *(1 mark)*

Q6 3 + 7 = **10** *(1 mark)*
20 + 60 is ten times bigger than 2 + 6.
2 + 6 = 8, so
20 + 60 = **80** *(1 mark)*

Q7 **5 faces** *(1 mark)*
**5 vertices** *(1 mark)*

Q8 2 + 2 + 2 + 1 = **7 bats** *(1 mark)*

Q9 **cm** should be circled. *(1 mark)*

Q10 *(1 mark)*

Q11 *(1 mark)*

Q12 You can check an addition by doing the opposite — a subtraction.
**79 − 56** or **79 − 23** *(1 mark)*

Q13 4 × 2 = 8
8 + 5 = **13** *(1 mark)*

Q14 15 ÷ 3 = **5 roses** *(1 mark)*

Q15 41 > 36 *(1 mark)*

Q16 **6** should be circled. *(1 mark)*
$\frac{1}{3}$ of 24 = 24 ÷ 3
= **8 sweets** *(1 mark)*

Q17 54 − 20 = 34
34 − 3 = **31** *(1 mark)*

## Section One — Number and Place Value

### Page 6 — Place Value

Q1 **3** *(1 mark)*
**7** *(1 mark)*

Q2 **7** *(1 mark)*
**0** *(1 mark)*

Q3 **4** *(1 mark)*
**1** *(1 mark)*

Q4 **571** or **517** *(1 mark)*
**157** or **751** *(1 mark)*

Q5 **30** *(1 mark)*

### Page 7 — Reading and Writing Numbers

Q1 **680** *(1 mark)*
**962** *(1 mark)*
**401** *(1 mark)*

Q2 **Seven hundred and nine** *(1 mark)*
**Two hundred and twenty two** *(1 mark)*
**One thousand** *(1 mark)*

Q3 4 + 5 = 9 = **nine** *(1 mark)*

### Page 8 — Counting in Multiples

Q1 4, **8**, **12**, 16, **20** *(1 mark)*

Q2 100, **200**, **300**, **400**, **500** *(1 mark)*

Q3 **100**, **500**, **250** *(1 mark)*

Q4 E.g. **24**, **12**
**200**, **150**
*(1 mark for 2 or 3 correct, 2 marks for all correct.)*

Q5 **8 / 16 / 24** *(1 mark)*
**4 / 12 / 20 / 28** *(1 mark)*

## Page 9 — 10 or 100 More or Less

Q1 **659** *(1 mark)*
**190** *(1 mark)*

Q2 **106** *(1 mark)*

Q3 **133** *(1 mark)*
**530** *(1 mark)*

Q4 **594** *(1 mark)*
**906** *(1 mark)*

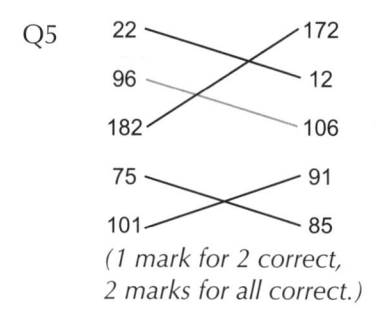

Q5 22 — 172
96 — 12
182 — 106
75 — 91
101 — 85
*(1 mark for 2 correct, 2 marks for all correct.)*

## Pages 10-11 — Ordering and Comparing Numbers

Q1 From smallest to largest:
**110 cm, 120 cm, 140 cm** *(1 mark)*

Q2 **Three hundred and fifty** *(1 mark)*

Q3 **One hundred and forty six** *(1 mark)*

Q4 From smallest to largest:
**218, 232, 651, 721, 729, 911** *(1 mark)*

Q5 From largest to smallest:
**159p, 153p, 98p** *(1 mark)*

Q6 21 °C < 23 °C
13 °C > 3 °C
7 °C > 5 °C
0 °C < 1 °C
*(1 mark for 2 correct, 2 marks for all correct.)*

Q7 7 + 11 > 6 + 4
6 + 8 = 7 + 7
5 + 8 > 2 + 9
9 − 8 < 9 − 6
*(1 mark for 2 or 3 correct, 2 marks for all correct.)*

# Answers

## Pages 12-13 — Partitioning

Q1  **367**
**119**
**735**
**258**
*(1 mark for 2 or 3 correct, 2 marks for all correct.)*

Q2  **400 + 30 + 8** *(1 mark)*
**600 + 50 + 2** *(1 mark)*
**100 + 0 + 9** *(1 mark)*

Q3  E.g. 250 + **50** + **100**
*(1 mark)*
E.g. 420 + **80** + **100**
*(1 mark)*
E.g. 680 + **20** + **300**
*(1 mark)*

Q4  51 + 46 = **50** + **1** + **40** + **6**
= **97** *(1 mark)*

22 + 67 = **20** + **2** + **60** + **7**
= **89** *(1 mark)*

Q5  17 = 10 + 7
21 = 20 + 1
20 + 10 = 30
7 + 1 = 8
30 + 8 = **38** *(1 mark)*

Q6  32 = 30 + 2
Mr Green has 2 boxes, so
30 + 30 = 60
2 + 2 = 4
60 + 4 = **64**
*(1 mark)*

Q7  14 = 10 + 4
20 + 10 = 30
30 + 4 = 34
34 + 6 = **40**
*(1 mark)*

## Pages 14-15 — Numbers on Scales

Q1  **30 g** *(1 mark)*

Q2  **24 cm** *(1 mark)*

Q3  **17 cm** *(1 mark)*

Q4  **21 °C** *(1 mark)*

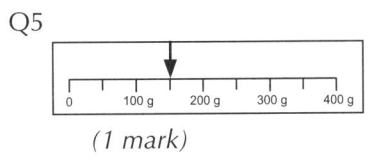

Q5  
```
          ↓
 |--|--|--|--|--|--|--|--|
 0   100 g  200 g  300 g  400 g
```
*(1 mark)*

Q6  **95 cm** *(1 mark)*

Q7  From left to right:
**210**, **250**
*(1 mark for each.)*

## Pages 16-17 — Solving Number Problems

Q1  55 = 50 + 5
32 = 30 + 2
50 + 30 = 80
5 + 2 = 7
80 + 7 = **87**
*(1 mark)*

Q2  **6** times
*(1 mark)*

Q3  750 = 700 + 50
250 = 200 + 50
700 + 200 = 900
50 + 50 = 100
900 + 100 = 1000
= **One thousand**
*(1 mark)*

Q4  The thermometer reads 38 °C, so the temperature needs to rise by **15 °C** to reach 53 °C. *(1 mark)*

Q5  225 > 218
105 < 194
34 > 20
89 < 99
*(1 mark for 2 or 3 correct, 2 marks for all correct.)*

Q6  115 + 100 = 215
35 = 30 + 5
215 + 30 = 245
245 + 5 = **250 g**
*(1 mark)*

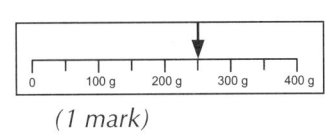

```
                    ↓
 |--|--|--|--|--|--|--|--|
 0   100 g  200 g  300 g  400 g
```
*(1 mark)*

**ANSWERS**

# Answers

## Section Two — Calculations

### Page 18 — Mental Addition

Q1  452 + 40 = **492** *(1 mark)*

Q2  324 + 4 = **328** *(1 mark)*
   241 + 500 = **741** *(1 mark)*
   716 + 70 = **786** *(1 mark)*

Q3  120 + **30** = 150
   **40** + 200 = 240
   **460** + 100 = 560
   30 + **140** = 170
   *(2 marks for all answers correct. Otherwise 1 mark for 3 answers correct.)*

Q4  **30**, **60** and **80** should be circled. *(1 mark)*

### Page 19 — Mental Subtraction

Q1  158 − 5 = **153** *(1 mark)*
   160 − 40 = **120** *(1 mark)*
   295 − 50 = **245** *(1 mark)*
   563 − 200 = **363** *(1 mark)*

Q2  689 − 70 = **619** *(1 mark)*

Q3  **340** and **430** should be circled. *(1 mark)*

Q4  **80** should be circled. *(1 mark)*

### Page 20 — Written Addition

Q1
```
   4 2 5
 + 1 3 4
 -------
   5 5 9
```
*(1 mark)*

Q2
```
   2 3 6
 + 2 5 0
 -------
   4 8 6
```
So she has **£486** *(1 mark)*

Q3
```
   1 8 6
 +   4 7
 -------
   2 3 3
   1 1
```
*(1 mark)*

Q4  Flower A:
```
    7 9
 +  1 8
 ------
    9 7
    1
```
**97 cm** *(1 mark)*

Flower B:
```
   1 2 8
 +   1 8
 -------
   1 4 6
     1
```
**146 cm** *(1 mark)*

### Page 21 — Written Subtraction

Q1
```
   6 8 8
 −   5 1
 -------
   6 3 7
```
*(1 mark)*

Q2
```
   9⁷8̶¹1
 − 6 7 2
 -------
   3 0 9
```
*(1 mark)*

Q3
```
   1 7 8
 − 1 1 5
 -------
   0 6 3
```
So Jake has **£63** more than Hannah. *(1 mark)*

Q4
```
   3⁷8̶¹1
 − 1 4 4
 -------
   2 3 7
```
**237 metres** *(1 mark)*

### Page 22 — The 3, 4 and 8 Times Tables

Q1  **56** *(1 mark)*

Q2  **24**, **32**, **16**, **8** and **20** should be circled. *(1 mark)*

Q3  5 × **8** = 40 *(1 mark)*
   12 × 3 = **36** *(1 mark)*

Q4  **18**, **21**, **15** and **36** should be circled. *(1 mark)*

Q5  8 bags of 3 cherries = 8 × 3 = 24 cherries. There is one left over. 24 + 1 = **25 cherries** *(1 mark)*

# Answers

## Pages 23-24 — Using Times Tables Facts

**Q1** E.g. 2 × 5 = 10
10 × 4 = **40** *(1 mark)*
E.g. 4 × 5 = 20
20 × 8 = **160** *(1 mark)*
E.g. 4 × 3 = 12
12 × 8 = **96** *(1 mark)*

**Q2** 8 × 6 = 48
So 8 × 60 = **480** *(1 mark)*
8 ÷ 2 = 4
So 80 ÷ 2 = **40** *(1 mark)*
27 ÷ 3 = **9** *(1 mark)*

**Q3** 40 × 3 = 120, so
120 ÷ 3 = **40** *(1 mark)*

**Q4** E.g. 45 = 30 + 15
30 ÷ 3 = 10
15 ÷ 3 = 5
10 + 5 = **15 sheep**
*(1 mark)*

**Q5** 60 × 4 = 240
240 ÷ 4 = **60** *(1 mark)*
50 × 6 = 300
300 ÷ 6 = **50** *(1 mark)*

**Q6** E.g. 34 = 30 + 4
30 × 4 = 120
4 × 4 = 16
120 + 16 = **136** *(1 mark)*
E.g. 25 = 20 + 5
20 × 8 = 160
5 × 8 = 40
160 + 40 = **200** *(1 mark)*
E.g. 49 = 40 + 9
40 × 3 = 120
9 × 3 = 27
120 + 27 = **147** *(1 mark)*

**Q7** 
    0 6 4
4 ⟌ 2²5¹6  *(1 mark)*

**Q8** 
    0 1 8
8 ⟌ 1 14⁶4
So each friend gets
**18 sweets** *(1 mark)*

## Page 25 — Estimating and Checking

**Q1** **26 + 17 = 43**
or **17 + 26 = 43** *(1 mark)*

**Q2** **2 × 49 = 98**
or **49 × 2 = 98** *(1 mark)*
**7 × 8 = 56**
or **8 × 7 = 56** *(1 mark)*

**Q3** Round each number to the nearest 10 to give **50 + 30**. *(1 mark)*
50 + 30 = **80**.
So 48 + 29 must be less than 80 because both numbers are smaller than the numbers used in the estimate. *(1 mark)*

**Q4** Estimate the correct answer using **140 ÷ 10 = 14**. 6 is much smaller than 14.
Or: **6 × 9 = 54**. 54 is much smaller than 137. *(1 mark)*

## Pages 26-27 — Solving Calculation Problems

**Q1** 36 ÷ 4 = **9 children**
*(1 mark)*

**Q2** 4 × 8 = 32
So 4 × 80 = **320 pence**
*(1 mark)*
7 × 8 = 56
So 7 × 80 = **560 pence**
*(1 mark)*

**Q3** 30 × 5 = **150 children**
*(1 mark)*

**Q4** E.g. 24 = 20 + 4
20 × 4 = 80
4 × 4 = 16
80 + 16 = **96 marbles**
*(1 mark)*
24 + 7 = 31
31 + 10 = **41 marbles**
*(1 mark)*

**Q5** E.g. 5 × £4 = £20
6 × £4 = £24
So he will be able to pay for it after **6 weeks**
*(1 mark)*
£24 − £23 = **£1** *(1 mark)*

**Q6** 9 − 2 = 7
7 × 3 = **21** *(1 mark)*

**Q7** 
    0 6 5
8 ⟌ 5⁵2⁴0
So 1 slice has a mass of
**65 g** *(1 mark)*

**Q8** E.g. 175 = 100 + 70 + 5
100 × 3 = 300
70 × 3 = 210
5 × 3 = 15
300 + 200 = 500
10 + 15 = 25
500 + 25 = **525 g**
*(1 mark)*

# Answers

## Section Three — Fractions

### Page 28 — Counting in Tenths

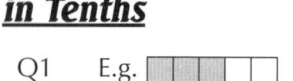

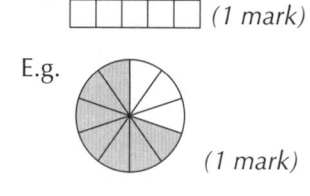

Q1  E.g. [shaded grid] *(1 mark)*

E.g. [shaded circle] *(1 mark)*

Q2  **C** *(1 mark)*

Q3  $\frac{4}{10}$ *(1 mark)*

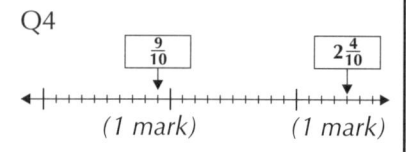

Q4  [number line with $\frac{9}{10}$ and $2\frac{4}{10}$ marked] *(1 mark) (1 mark)*

### Page 29 — Equivalent Fractions

Q1  E.g. [shaded circle] *(1 mark)*

E.g. [shaded bar] *(1 mark)*

Q2  E.g. $\frac{3}{4}$ *(1 mark)*

Q3  $\frac{6}{12}$ *(1 mark)*

E.g. $\frac{3}{6}, \frac{1}{2}$ *(1 mark)*

Q4  $\frac{2}{12}$ should be circled. *(1 mark)*

### Pages 30-31 — Ordering Fractions

Q1  $\frac{1}{12}, \frac{4}{12}, \frac{5}{12}, \frac{8}{12}, \frac{11}{12}$
*(1 mark for all correct.)*

Q2  $\frac{1}{10}, \frac{1}{7}, \frac{1}{6}, \frac{1}{3}, \frac{1}{2}$
*(1 mark for all correct.)*

Q3  $\frac{4}{12}, \frac{1}{10}, \frac{1}{6}$ and $\frac{1}{4}$ should be circled.
*(2 marks for all correct, otherwise 1 mark for 3 correct.)*

Q4  $\frac{1}{5}$ is bigger than $\frac{1}{9}$ and $\frac{1}{10}$ so **Matthew** won the most races. *(1 mark)*

Q5  $\frac{1}{4}$ *(1 mark)*

E.g. $\frac{2}{3}$ or $\frac{3}{4}$ *(1 mark)*

Q6  $\frac{2}{6}$ should be circled. *(1 mark)*

E.g. $\frac{2}{6}$ is equivalent to $\frac{1}{3}$. $\frac{1}{3}$ is bigger than $\frac{1}{4}$ because the whole is divided into fewer parts. *(1 mark)*

### Pages 32-33 — Adding and Subtracting Fractions

Q1  [shaded grid] $= \frac{15}{16}$ *(1 mark)*

[shaded circle] $= \frac{4}{9}$ *(1 mark)*

Q2  $\frac{1}{5} + \frac{3}{5} = \frac{4}{5}$ *(1 mark)*

$\frac{5}{10} + \frac{2}{10} = \frac{7}{10}$ *(1 mark)*

$\frac{1}{3} + \frac{1}{3} = \frac{2}{3}$ *(1 mark)*

$\frac{2}{8} + \frac{4}{8} = \frac{6}{8}$ *(1 mark)*

Q3  $\frac{5}{7} - \frac{2}{7} = \frac{3}{7}$ *(1 mark)*

$\frac{9}{10} - \frac{4}{10} = \frac{5}{10}$ *(1 mark)*

Q4  $\frac{7}{9} - \frac{3}{9} = \frac{4}{9}$ *(1 mark)*

Q5  $\frac{5}{15} + \frac{9}{15} = \frac{14}{15}$ *(1 mark)*

Q6  $\frac{4}{10} - \frac{3}{10} = \frac{1}{10}$ *(1 mark)*

$\frac{2}{5} + \frac{1}{5} = \frac{3}{5}$ *(1 mark)*

Q7  [shaded grid] $= \frac{7}{12}$
*(1 mark)*

### Pages 34-35 — Fractions of Amounts

Q1  **18** should be circled *(1 mark)*

Q2  $24 \div 4 = $ **6** *(1 mark)*

Q3  $12 \div 3 = $ **4 snails** *(1 mark)*

Q4  $16 \div 8 = 2$
$2 \times 3 = $ **6 squares**
*(1 mark)*

Q5  $20 \div 4 = 5$
$5 \times 3 = $ **15 sweets**
*(1 mark)*

Q6  $40 \div 10 = 4$ given away.
$40 - 4 = $ **36 marbles**
*(1 mark)*

Q7  $56 \div 8 = 7$
$7 \times 5 = 35$
So **35** should be circled.
*(1 mark)*

Q8  $40 \div 4 = 10$
$10 \times 3 = $ **30** *(1 mark)*
$9 \div 3 = 3$
$3 \times 2 = $ **6** *(1 mark)*
$30 \div 5 = 6$
$6 \times 4 = $ **24** *(1 mark)*

Q9  $\frac{1}{5}$ is $30 \div 5 = 6$ cm.
$\frac{2}{5} = 2 \times 6 = $ **12 cm**
*(1 mark)*

# Answers

## Pages 36-37 — Solving Fraction Problems

Q1  **4/9** *(1 mark)*

Q2  The whole book is $\frac{10}{10}$.
$\frac{10}{10} - \frac{4}{10} = \frac{6}{10}$ *(1 mark)*

Q3  12 ÷ 4 = **£3** *(1 mark)*
12 ÷ 3 = **£4** *(1 mark)*

Q4  The whole of Chloe's hair is $\frac{5}{5}$. $\frac{5}{5} - \frac{2}{5} = \frac{3}{5}$ *(1 mark)*

Q5  32 ÷ 8 = 4
4 × 3 = 12 kg given away.
32 − 12 = **20 kg** *(1 mark)*

Q6  $\frac{2}{9} + \frac{2}{9} + \frac{2}{9} + \frac{2}{9} = \frac{8}{9}$
*(1 mark)*

Q7  One half of **18** is 9.
*(1 mark)*
One third of **30** is 10.
*(1 mark)*
**One quarter** of 12 is 3.
*(1 mark)*

Q8  $\frac{1}{3}$ is equivalent to $\frac{2}{6}$.
$\frac{2}{6} + \frac{1}{6} = \frac{3}{6}$ eaten in total.
The whole pizza is $\frac{6}{6}$.
$\frac{6}{6} - \frac{3}{6} = \frac{3}{6}$ **left** *(1 mark)*

Q9  $\frac{1}{4}$ of 24 = 24 ÷ 4 = 6
So $\frac{1}{2}$ of ☐ = 6
The opposite of ÷2 is ×2, so ☐ = 6 × 2 = **12**
*(1 mark)*

## Section Four — Measurement

### Pages 38-39 — Length, Mass and Volume

Q1  **30 mm, 50 mm** *(1 mark)*

Q2  **3000 ml, 2 m** *(1 mark)*

Q3  220 × 10 = 2200 mm
So **220 cm** is the longest.
*(1 mark)*

Q4  524 + 400 = 924
924 + 70 = 994
994 + 6 = 1000 g
So 524 + 476 = 1000 g
1000 g = **1 kg** *(1 mark)*

Q5  2 kg = 2000 g.
2000 g = 20 × 100 g.
So there are **20 shapes**.
*(1 mark)*

Q6  **74 mm**
*(1 mark)*

Q7  Amount of water in the container starts at 450 ml.
450 ml − 250 ml = **200 ml**
*(1 mark)*

Q8  2 m = 200 cm
200 cm = 4 × 50 cm
So Saba needs **4 tiles** to make a line 2 m long.
*(1 mark)*

Q9  12 × 100 ml = 1200 ml
2 l = 2000 ml
2000 ml − 1200 ml
= **800 ml**
*(2 marks for correct answer.
Otherwise 1 mark for 12 × 100 ml = 1200 ml.)*

## Pages 40-41 — Perimeter

Q1  4 + 2 + 4 + 2 = **12 m**
*(1 mark)*

Q2  3 + 3 + 4 = **10 cm**
*(1 mark)*

Q3  2 + 3 + 5 + 1 + 4 = **15 cm**
*(1 mark)*

Q4  2 + 1 + 2 + 1 + 2 = **8 mm**
*(1 mark)*

Q5  Possible answers are:

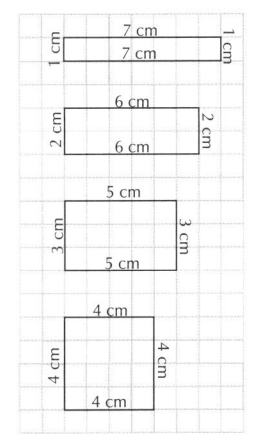

*(1 mark for one of these.)*

Q6  5 + 1 + 3 + 6 + 3 + 1
= **19 cm** *(1 mark)*

Q7  4 × 8 = **32 cm** *(1 mark)*

**ANSWERS**

# Answers

## Page 42 — Money

Q1  95 − 3 = 92p
    92 − 50 = **42p** *(1 mark)*

Q2  £1.20 + 85p
    120 + 5 = 125p
    125 + 80 = 205p
    £2.05 + 75p
    205 + 5 = 210p
    210 + 70 = 280p
    = **£2.80** *(1 mark)*
    **Yes**, he has enough money. *(1 mark)*

Q3  205 + 7 = 212
    212 + 20 = 232
    232 + 100 = 332p
    = **£3.32** *(1 mark)*

    200 − 5 = 195
    195 − 40 = 155
    155 − 100 = **55p**
    *(1 mark)*

## Page 43 — Clocks

Q1  a) **8:23**
    b) **11:33**
    c) **4:50**
    d) **6:07**
    *(1 mark for 2 or 3 correct, 2 marks for all correct.)*

Q2  Ten past one *(1 mark)*
    Twenty past seven *(1 mark)*

Q3  1 minute = 60 seconds
    60 + 60 = **120 seconds**
    *(1 mark)*

Q4  January: **31**
    September: **30**
    A leap year: **366**
    February: **28**
    *(1 mark for 2 or 3 correct, 2 marks for 4 correct.)*

## Pages 44-45 — Time Problems

Q1  9 pm to 12 am
    = 3 hours.
    12 am + 6 hours
    = **6 am**
    *(1 mark)*

Q2  
| Leaves from London | 1:00 | 2:20 | 3:20 |
| Arrives in Bristol | 2:30 | 3:50 | 4:50 |

*(1 mark for each correct.)*

Q3  10.15 to 11.00 is 45 mins
    11.00 to 11.06 is 6 mins
    45 + 6 = **51 mins**
    *(1 mark)*

    10.23 to 10.30 is 7 mins
    10.30 to 10.49 is 19 mins
    7 + 19 = **26 mins**
    *(1 mark)*

Q4  Andrew leaves the house at 4:10.
    He arrives at the park at 4:45.
    So it takes him **35 minutes** to walk to the park.
    *(1 mark)*

Q5  9:00 am — 5:30 pm
    = **8½ hours** *(1 mark)*
    The shortest opening is on **Wednesday** when the shop is open from
    9:00 am — 1:00 pm
    = 4 hours. *(1 mark)*
    12.55 pm — 1.30 pm
    = **35 minutes** *(1 mark)*

## Section Five — Geometry

## Pages 46-47 — 2D Shapes

Q1  — triangle
    — hexagon
    — heptagon
    *(1 mark)*

Q2  E.g.
    *(1 mark for any shape with five straight sides drawn.)*

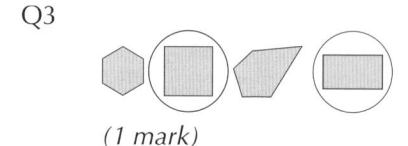

Q3  *(1 mark)*

Q4  **3** *(1 mark)*
    **3** *(1 mark)*

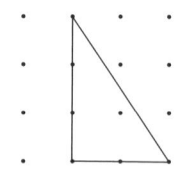

Q5  E.g.
    *(1 mark for any right-angled triangle drawn.)*

ANSWERS

# Answers

Q6 square *(1 mark)*
irregular hexagon *(1 mark)*

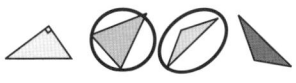

Q7 *(1 mark for both triangles correct.)*

## Pages 48-49 — 3D Shapes

Q1 cube, sphere, cone *(1 mark for all three answers correct.)*

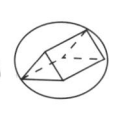

Q2 *(1 mark)*

Q3 sphere — no flat surfaces
tetrahedron — each face is a triangle
cube — has six faces
*(1 mark for all three answers correct.)*

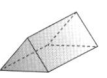

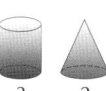

Q4 6  5  3  2
*(1 mark for all four answers correct.)*

Q5 **8** sticks *(1 mark)*
**5** balls of clay *(1 mark)*

Q6 **6** edges *(1 mark)*

Q7 cylinder *(1 mark)*
cuboid *(1 mark)*

## Pages 50-51 — Angles and Lines

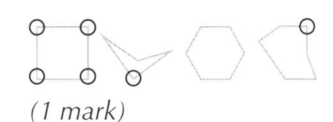

Q1 *(1 mark)*

Q2 **4** *(1 mark)*

Q3 Angles **X** and **Y** should be circled. *(1 mark)*

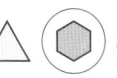

Q4 *(1 mark for both shapes with parallel lines circled.)*

Q5 **z** *(1 mark)*
**v** *(1 mark)*
**v** *(1 mark)*

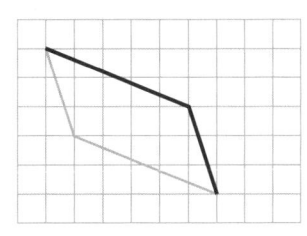

Q6 *(1 mark. Both lines must be correct.)*

## Section Six — Statistics

### Page 52 — Tables

Q1

| Animal | Tally | Frequency |
|---|---|---|
| Cat | 𝍲 I | 6 |
| Dog | IIII | 4 |
| Rabbit | II | 2 |

*(1 mark)*
4 − 2 = 2, so there are **2** more dogs than rabbits. *(1 mark)*

Q2

| Bird | Tally | Frequency |
|---|---|---|
| blackbird | 𝍲 I | 6 |
| crow | 𝍲 IIII | 9 |
| sparrow | IIII | 4 |
| starling | 𝍲 𝍲 𝍲 I | 16 |

*(1 mark)*
6 + 9 + 4 + 16 = 35, so there were **35** birds in total. *(1 mark)*

Q3

| Colour | Tally |
|---|---|
| Blue | 𝍲 II |
| Red | 𝍲 III |
| Silver | 𝍲 |

*(1 mark)*

### Page 53 — Bar Charts

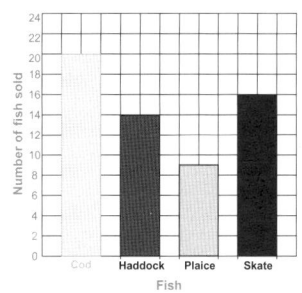

Q1 *(1 mark)*
20 + 14 + 9 + 16
= **59 fish** *(1 mark)*

Q2 **Ready salted** *(1 mark)*
**11 packets** *(1 mark)*
11 + 13 + 8 + 14
= **46 packets** *(1 mark)*

# Answers

## Page 54 — Pictograms

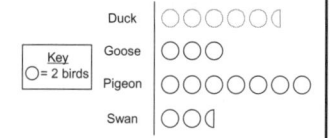

Q1 
| | |
|---|---|
| Duck | ○○○○○◐ |
| Goose | ○○◐ |
| Pigeon | ○○○○○○○ |
| Swan | ○○◐ |

Key: ○ = 2 birds

*(2 marks if all correct, otherwise 1 mark for just two rows of circles correct.)*

**9 starlings** *(1 mark)*
**8½ circles** *(1 mark)*

## Page 55 — Interpreting Tables and Charts

Q1 **25 pigs** *(1 mark)*
35 − 15 = **20** *(1 mark)*

Q2 22 + 14 + 16 + 24 = **76 girls** *(1 mark)*
24 − 14 = **10 girls** *(1 mark)*

## Pages 56-59 — Year Three Objectives Test

Q1 **24**, **32** and **48** *(1 mark)*

Q2 36 ÷ 3 = **12** *(1 mark)*

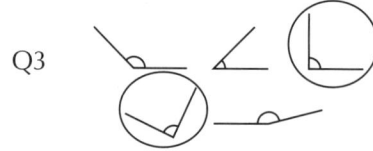

Q3 *(1 mark for each correctly circled angle.)*

Q4 3 × 4 = 12
20 − 8 = 12
**8** *(1 mark)*

Q5 54 ÷ **9** = 6 *(1 mark)*
54 − 36 = **18** *(1 mark)*

Q6 Team A scored 2 + 1 = **3** goals. *(1 mark)*
Team B scored 8 − 5 = **3** more goals than Team C. *(1 mark)*

Q7 87 = 80 + 7
178 − 7 = 171
171 − 80 = **91** *(1 mark)*

Q8 13 = 10 + 3
10 × 4 = 40
3 × 4 = 12
40 + 12 = **52** *(1 mark)*

Q9 **40 minutes** *(1 mark)*

Q10 **A** *(1 mark)*

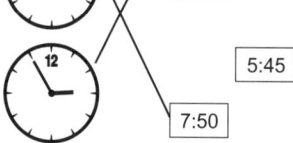

Q11 *(1 mark for 1 or 2 correct, 2 marks for all 3 correct.)*

Q12 **6 boxes shaded**, e.g:

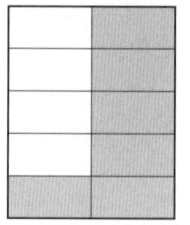

*(1 mark)*

Q13 $\frac{1}{3}$ of 33 = 33 ÷ 3 = 11
11 × 2 = 22
11 = $\frac{1}{2}$ of **22** *(1 mark)*

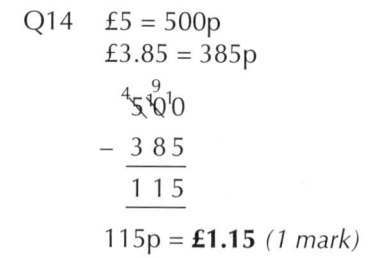

Q14 £5 = 500p
£3.85 = 385p

```
  4 9
  5̷ 0̷ ¹0
−   3 8 5
─────────
    1 1 5
```

115p = **£1.15** *(1 mark)*

Q15 3 × 3 **>** 2 × 4
6 × 4 **=** 8 × 3
5 × 4 **<** 7 × 3
*(1 mark for 2 answers correct, 2 marks for all answers correct.)*